USAFE

IN THE 1980s

Adrian Symonds

AMBERLEY

Acknowledgements

I would like to thank Sally Tunnicliffe for her assistance and keen eye for detail. Special thanks go to my wife, Louise, and son, Charlie, for their support and patience.

This book is dedicated to the men and women of the United States Air Force who travelled across an ocean to help defend Western Europe during the Cold War.

First published 2020

Amberley Publishing
The Hill, Stroud
Gloucestershire, GL5 4EP

www.amberley-books.com

Copyright © Adrian Symonds, 2020

The right of Adrian Symonds to be identified as the Author of this work has been asserted in accordance with the Copyrights, Designs and Patents Act 1988.

ISBN 978 1 4456 9854 0 (print)
ISBN 978 1 4456 9855 7 (ebook)

British Library Cataloguing in Publication Data. A catalogue record for this book is available from the British Library.

Typesetting by Aura Technology and Software Services, India. Printed in the UK.

Contents

Introduction

In the aftermath of the 1979 Soviet invasion of Afghanistan, East-West détente shuddered to a halt, whilst President Reagan's 1981 arrival in office resulted in an unprecedented peacetime military build-up. Cold War tensions between the United States and the Soviet Union, and their respective North Atlantic Treaty Organisation (NATO) and Warsaw Pact (WarPac) allies, rose to their highest levels.

The United States Air Forces in Europe (USAFE) in the last decade of the Cold War was a huge organisation, holding 700 combat aircraft. It had 57,000 personnel, augmented by a further 24,000 personnel from other USAF commands deployed to Europe to support USAFE, supported by 11,000 US and European workers, plus 69,000 military dependents. During the decade a new class of weapons system, nuclear Ground Launched Cruise Missiles, joined USAFE. On the Cold War front line, USAFE had been upgrading its capabilities since the late 1970s. Whilst it had been largely equipped with variants of the venerable F-4 Phantom II, in 1977 USAFE doubled its F-111 strike fleet by converting a wing to the F-111F, adding to an existing F-111E wing. That year the F-15A/B Eagle entered USAFE service, followed in 1978 by the A-10A Thunderbolt II. The majority of the remaining F-4 fleet (apart from specialist variants, the last such variant, F-4G, reaching USAFE in 1979) would be supplanted by F-16 Fighting Falcons during the 1980s.

USAFE serves both US national and NATO interests; therefore, the Command concentrated upon the threat from the Soviet and WarPac forces to the east. However, the 1980s rise of international terrorism became another preoccupation of the Reagan administration; consequently, when USAFE finally flew in anger it was against a very different foe.

Seen deployed to Zaragoza Air Base, Spain, during 1986 are, front-to-back: a 493rd TFS, 48th TFW, F-111F; a 509th TFS, 81st TFW, A-10A; a 525th TFS, 36th TFW, F-15C; a 81st TFS, 52nd TFW, F-4E; a 496th TFS, 50th TFW, F-16A; and a 527th AS, 10th TRW, F-5E. (National Archives and Records Administration)

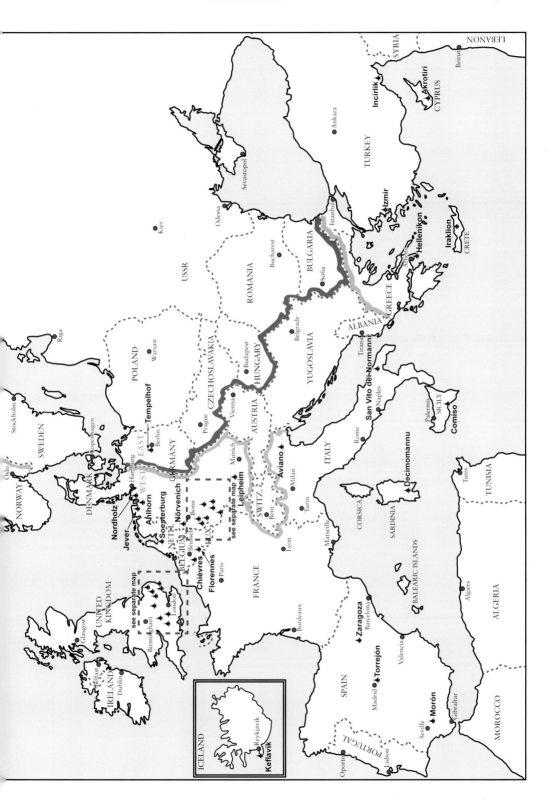

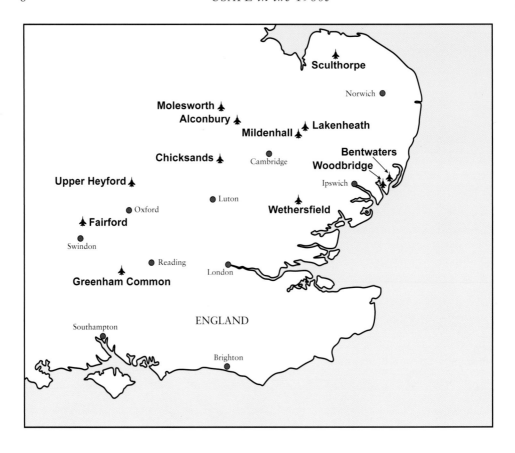

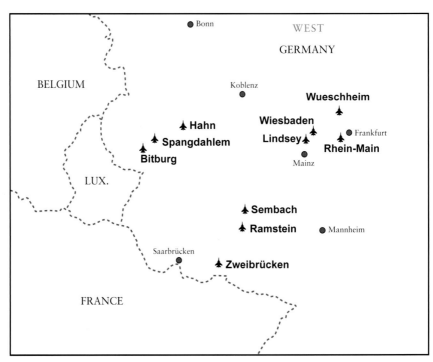

NATO and the Warsaw Pact

NATO Command

NATO-declared allied air, sea and land forces, including USAFE, not only had national administrative structures, but were also integrated into parallel NATO operational command structures. The most important NATO command was Allied Command Europe (ACE).

Under ACE was Allied Forces Central Europe (AFCENT) – overseeing Northern Army Group (NORTHAG, controlling NATO forces defending northern West Germany), Central Army Group (CENTAG, controlling forces defending southern West Germany) – and Allied Air Forces Central Europe (AAFCE) – overseeing Second Allied Tactical Air Force (2 ATAF, directing NATO air units supporting NORTHAG) and Fourth Allied Tactical Air Force (4 ATAF, directing NATO air units supporting CENTAG). Therefore, USAFE units based in southern West Germany (Seventeenth Air Force) would in wartime have fallen under 4 ATAF. Furthermore, in wartime the Seventeenth Air Force commander became 4 ATAF Commander. USAF aircraft reinforcing northern West Germany in wartime would fall under 2 ATAF.

ACE also controlled Allied Forces Northern Europe (AFNORTH, controlling forces in Norway, Denmark and northernmost West Germany), and in southern Europe Allied Forces Southern Europe (AFSOUTH). AFSOUTH included Allied Air Forces Southern Europe (AIRSOUTH), controlling 5 ATAF – with wartime control of NATO air units in Italy – and 6 ATAF – with wartime control of NATO air units in Greece and Turkey. USAF units deploying to these areas in wartime would fall under these commands.

Furthermore, ACE controlled United Kingdom Air Forces (including USAFE Third Air Force units and any other USAF units in, or passing through, the UK during wartime), the NATO Airborne Early Warning Force (controlling the multi-national NATO E-3 Sentry force) and the ACE Mobile Force (a multinational quick reaction force that could be quickly despatched anywhere in ACE's command area).

The Threat

The Soviets and their allies maintained a vast military machine with the means to invade Western Europe. Any invasion of the West might have started with little notice, perhaps with preparations disguised as a large-scale exercise (as they had done when invading their errant 'ally' Czechoslovakia in 1968) or it may have been a bolt from the barracks. It could have started after a period of increasing tensions, with both sides fully deployed in the field. However it started, it would have been a massive onslaught, almost definitely involving tactical nuclear weapons.

Soviet and WarPac tank and motorised rifle divisions would have poured into West Germany from East Germany, Czechoslovakia and Poland, followed by even larger reinforcements from the Soviet Union.

NATO had eighteen heavy divisions in West Germany, rising to thirty divisions if all of the units not based in Germany in peacetime, but committed to the defence (Belgian, British, Canadian, Dutch and US), arrived in time to meet the attack. US-based reinforcements were planned to be able to move from the US to Germany within ten days. This, known as Return of Forces to Germany ('Reforger'), relied on airlifting personnel to Europe, where they would meet up with prepositioned equipment: 'Prepositioning Of Materiel Configured in Unit Sets' or 'POMCUS'.

Soviet and WarPac forces had fifty-five in-place heavy divisions, which within thirty days of mobilising would be joined by a further eighty-three, for a total of 138 divisions. They had around 20,150 tanks in Central Europe, whilst reinforcing divisions from the western USSR would add a further 21,145 tanks within thirty days of mobilisation. Facing this NATO had 13,750 in place, with a further 1,900 available from the US, France and the UK, within thirty days of mobilisation. It is no wonder that overwhelming waves of Soviet tanks, large numbers of other armoured vehicles, plus hundreds of Mi-24 attack helicopters swarming overhead, was the abiding nightmarish image in the minds of NATO planners.

The likely scenario, indicated by plans and exercises revealed post-Cold War, would have been as follows:

To the north, whilst WarPac navies forced their way through the Kattegat and Skagerrak straits into the North Sea, an amphibious and airborne landing (three divisions and two regiments) would have been conducted against Denmark.

Another small thrust (five divisions) would launch across Jutland, north of Hamburg, cutting Denmark and most of Schleswig-Holstein off from the rest of West Germany.

The three main thrusts would have been on the Central Front. The northernmost of these (nine divisions) would pass to the south of Hamburg, aiming for the Channel coast, cutting off NATO supply lines. Five NATO divisions and two brigades would face them if they all arrived in time.

Further south, nine divisions would have struck through the Hanover area, aiming for the Ruhr. This thrust would encounter three British divisions, plus possibly one West German division. Alternatively, it may have been directed further south, to take advantage of the relatively weak Belgian units in the sector to the south.

The southernmost of the main thrusts (seven divisions) would have been through the Fulda Gap, heading to Frankfurt. This may subsequently have swung north towards the Ruhr and the US POMCUS sites near the Dutch border. Three NATO divisions, a brigade and an armoured cavalry regiment defended this sector.

Further supporting thrusts would have taken place further south, three divisions passing through the Meiningen Gap heading for Stuttgart, hitting the two divisions and armoured cavalry regiment in the sector.

NATO's defence of the Czech/West German border was relatively light compared to sectors further north, with just two divisions, possibly reinforced by a brigade. From Czechoslovakia seven WarPac divisions would cross the northern section of the Czech/West German frontier heading for Nuremberg, carrying on to Stuttgart or swinging south towards Munich.

Finally, six divisions would strike near the junction of the West German/Czech/Austrian borders, possibly swinging through neutral Austria, moving on to Munich after hitting the West Germans in the flank.

There were contingency plans for an additional thrust (ten divisions) from Hungary, cutting through neutral Austria into southern West Germany, striking the stretched NATO forces in the right and rear.

Helicopter-borne air assaults would have captured key points ahead of these attacking armies, with troops carried in Mi-8 and Mi-6 helicopters, supported by Mi-24 attack helicopters – 330 of the latter were in Soviet Army Aviation units in East Germany alone. Mi-24s would also attack battlefield targets, supporting the armour sweeping forward.

The Soviets planned to use 233 tactical nuclear weapons during an initial strike on forward positions, followed by a further 294. During the 1980s Soviet doctrine officially moved away from nuclear offense to conventional defence. Whilst this ended Soviet intentions to make first use of nuclear weapons, the new 'defensive' doctrine remained distinctly 'offensive', with a massive conventional counterattack on NATO.

The Soviet shift to conventional doctrine meant that combat aircraft took on increased importance for neutralising NATO air power – hitherto the role of tactical nuclear missiles.

During the 1980s, the Soviets narrowed the technological gap, whilst maintaining their quantitative advantage, notably within their air forces. The large numbers of MiG-29s and Su-27s that entered service were a major concern to NATO. The latest versions of Su-17, Su-24 and MiG-27 strike/attack aircraft were similar in capability to their Western equivalents. The Su-25 provided highly effective Close Air Support (CAS), whilst specialist types like the MiG-25BM Suppression of Enemy Air Defences (SEAD) and Su-24MP Electronic Countermeasures (ECM) jets provided improved ability to penetrate NATO air defences.

WarPac air support would have been as impressive as their ground assault. The key unit for WarPac air forces was the regiment, equivalent to the USAF wing, but generally smaller. Nominally composed of three squadrons of fifteen aircraft, in reality combat aircraft regiments generally held thirty-five to forty aircraft. In wartime a fourth squadron was intended to be added to each regiment, bringing it theoretically to sixty aircraft.

Soviet 'Frontal Aviation' units in East Germany, Czechoslovakia, Poland and Hungary, along with the air forces of those WarPac countries, contained thirty fighter regiments with *c.* 1,050 aircraft. There were six Su-24 strike regiments (plus three regiments detached in the Baltic) with *c.* 315 aircraft, three Su-25 CAS regiments (*c.* 105 aircraft) and twenty-two other ground attack regiments (with *c.* 770 MiG-21/-23BN/-27s and Su-7/-17/-22s). There were also eight tactical reconnaissance regiments (*c.* 280 aircraft). These would be quickly augmented by large-scale reinforcements from the Soviet Union.

Whilst their heavy bombers would likely be reserved for strategic targets, Soviet Long Range Aviation's medium bombers were also available – the 46th Air Army's nine (Tu-16K, Tu-22K and Tu-22M) bomber regiments and two (Tu-16R/Tu-22R) reconnaissance regiments.

PVO (air defence organisation) regiments would likely have deployed from their bases in the USSR to central Europe, defending WarPac airspace, freeing the bulk of the Soviet and WarPac fighters to concentrate on the air superiority mission in NATO airspace. PVO units in the western USSR were equipped in 1980 with the Su-9/-11/-15, MiG-23P/-23M/-25P and Yak-28P; by 1989 their equipment had been upgraded to the MiG-23P/-23M/-23MLD/-25PD/-31 and Su-15TM/-27P.

Soviet/WarPac air forces planned to establish three air sectors (north, central and south), each containing three 'air corridors' via which their combat aircraft would punch through NATO air defences. Each of these nine air corridors would have been 25 miles wide and 100 miles long. To create these corridors, initially a fighter sweep would have been conducted to tackle NATO fighters and to seek to destroy E-3 AEW aircraft. Priority ground targets (radar stations, SAM sites, etc.) would have been hit by airstrikes, tactical missiles and Spetsnaz special forces teams. Mi-8 helicopter ECM variants would jam radars and communications. Further jamming would be conducted by ground stations, plus An-12BK-PPS ECM aircraft flying just behind friendly lines; these would also lay chaff corridors near the front, through which MiG-25BM SEAD aircraft and other strike jets (Su-17s/Su-24s/MiG-27s) could approach to knock out NATO air defences. Su-24MP, Yak-28PP and Tu-16SPS/Tu-16P ECM aircraft would escort these strikes. Tu-16 Yolka/Tu-16E chaff-laying aircraft would extend the chaff corridor into NATO airspace, through which the An-12BK-PPS would pass to extend its jamming. This whole endeavour would be heavily escorted by fighters.

Assuming 80 per cent availability of Soviet/WarPac Central Front aircraft, there would have been *c.* 840 air superiority/escort fighters, *c.* 420 Su-24 strike aircraft, *c.* 85 Su-25 CAS aircraft, *c.* 620 other ground attack jets and *c.* 225 tactical

NATO air power in West Germany during 1987. A USAFE F-15C from the 22nd TFS, 36th TFW, from Bitburg AB leads an RAF Germany Tornado GR Mk 1 from No. 14 Squadron based at RAF Brüggen and a Luftwaffe Tornado IDS from Jagdbombergeschwader 32 based at Lechfeld AB. (NARA)

reconnaissance aircraft initially available. Also available were *c.* 250 Tu-16, Tu-22K and Tu-22M medium bombers and *c.* 55 reconnaissance Tu-16/22 aircraft. Very small numbers of essential SEAD and ECM aircraft would support these combat aircraft.

Around 2,500 aircraft would have created, and pushed through, these nine corridors in an initial strike. Each of the three sectors would be transited by around 280 air superiority fighters, 140 Su-24 strike aircraft, 200 other ground attack jets, 75 tactical reconnaissance aircraft and 100 medium bombers/reconnaissance bombers. Once through the corridors they would split up and make their way to their respective targets in West Germany and beyond. Meanwhile, over the battlefield would also be the Su-25s and Mi-24s directly supporting the armoured thrusts on the ground. The plan was to sustain three such waves in each of the three sectors (therefore nine waves in total) per day, after an initial surge of eight waves per sector (for a total of thirty-two waves) during the first day or so. The above aircraft would no doubt face heavy attrition, but this would soon be offset by reinforcements from the western USSR. Facing these WarPac air forces, in peacetime NATO maintained around 1,350 combat aircraft in Central Europe, courtesy of the Belgian, Danish, Netherlands and West German Air Forces plus RAF Germany and 17 AF of USAFE. However, these would have been considerably reinforced in wartime.

NATO faced daunting odds. A key role for NATO air forces early in any conflict was to slow up the advance of WarPac ground forces, whilst striking the follow-on forces that were approaching to reinforce the front, buying time for NATO forces in Germany to deploy and for reinforcements from overseas to arrive.

USAFE in Detail

The Second World War 'United States Strategic Air Forces in Europe' became 'United States Air Forces in Europe' on 7 August 1945. The developing Cold War saw its first major incident during the 1948/49 Berlin Blockade and airlift, whilst the United States and eleven other Western nations signed the North Atlantic Treaty on 4 April 1949, creating NATO.

The Cold War first turned hot with the 1950 onset of the Korean War. However, the Truman Administration gave a higher priority to Europe than Korea as it expanded its forces due to the Soviet threat. During the early 1950s thirteen aircraft wings were deployed from the United States to bases in France, the United Kingdom and West Germany, joining USAFE.

This vast expansion required the activation of several numbered air forces under USAFE to administer the units. In 1951 Third Air Force activated to control USAFE units in the United Kingdom, and Twelfth Air Force to control units in France and West Germany. In 1953 Seventeenth Air Force was established, controlling F-86F units defending SAC bases in French Morocco and having responsibility for activities throughout the Mediterranean, North Africa, southern Europe and into Asia. USAF units left (now independent) Morocco in 1963.

In 1959 nuclear-armed USAF units were asked to leave France, relocating to West Germany and the UK; President de Gaulle expelled remaining USAFE units from France in 1966.

After several reorganisations, by 1966 USAFE's structure was: Third Air Force controlling units in the UK, Sixteenth Air Force controlling units in Southern Europe, the Mediterranean and into Asia, and Seventeenth Air Force controlling units in Central Europe. This structure persisted into the 1980s and beyond.

It is important to note that, whilst space dictates that this title only covers combat and other flying units, there are (as for all USAF commands) many non-flying units throughout USAFE. The majority of personnel would have served in non-flying units, examples including Special Security, Civil Engineering, Air Postal, School, Computer Services, Field Printing, Management Engineering and Materiel squadrons. Even within the various wings which will be detailed, as well as the flying squadrons noted, there were also various supporting units including Aircraft Generation, Component Repair and Equipment Maintenance squadrons. There was also the wing command post as well as offices and units for intelligence, weapons and tactics, plans and standardisation-evaluation ('stan/eval').

Third Air Force

Headquartered at RAF Mildenhall, England, Third Air Force (3 AF) controlled United Kingdom-based units.

A 55th TFS, 20th TFW F-111E drops inert Mk 82 practice bombs (formally known as BDU-50s) over a British bombing range during 1983. (NARA)

The main hitting power came courtesy of two F-111 wings. Their wartime role was striking targets deep behind the Iron Curtain from their British bases, including 'counter-air' (hitting WarPac airfields), as well as other installations, supply dumps, communications and follow-on ground forces approaching the front. F-111s provided NATO's longest-ranged tactical strike capability, by the 1980s sharing the role with West Germany-based RAF and Luftwaffe Tornados. However, F-111s flying from UK bases could penetrate deeper (at higher speeds) into Eastern Europe than Tornados could from their West German bases closer to the front. This capability was not lost on the Soviets; in the first round of 1970s Strategic Arms Limitation Talks, the F-111 was the only aircraft type that they specifically raised and consequently the F-111 was treated as a 'strategic' weapons system in these talks.

F-111s featured Terrain-Following Radar (TFR) integrated into the automatic flight control system, allowing for 'hands-off' flight down to 200 feet at high speeds (still a rare capability by the 1980s).

USAFE F-111E models relied on 'dumb' bombs for conventional attacks. Twenty-four could be carried on wing pylons, but typical loads (for the best balance between payload and range) were eight high-drag 750 lb cluster bombs (e.g. CBU-87 anti-personnel/incendiary and CBU-89 anti-armour/anti-personnel) or alternatively eight/twelve low-drag general-purpose (LDGP) Mk 82 bombs. Other options included 2,000 lb Mk 84s and BLU-107 Durandel anti-runway penetration bombs. In order to deliver Mk 82/84 bombs at low level, high-drag bomb tail kits converted them into retarded bombs, slowing their descent, allowing the aircraft time to clear the bomb's blast zone. Vietnam-era Snakeye Mk 82 kits, featuring drag-inducing 'petals' which popped out after release, required the aircraft to reduce speed before releasing. The later Air Inflatable Retard (AIR) kit could be fitted to either the Mk 82 or Mk 84; its hybrid balloon/parachute 'ballute' allowed release at much higher speeds. The AN/ALQ-131 'shallow' ECM pod was carried for self-defence whilst AIM-9P-3 Sidewinder air-to-air missiles (AAMs) were an option (more effective AIM-9L/Ms, having larger rear fins, would not fit on the wing outboard shoulder pylons).

Above: A pair of F-111Es from the 55th TFS (nearest) and 79th TFS (furthest) over their RAF Upper Heyford base during 1983. They are carrying inert Mk 82 practice bombs outboard and SUU-21 practice bomb dispensers inboard. The SUU-21 was developed as a safety precaution for USAFE aircraft use; it carried the practice bombs within an enclosed bomb bay (unlike the earlier SUU-20 dispensers, in which the practice bombs were carried exposed) and they were spring ejected – this added safety was needed due to the requirement to fly more regularly over populated areas in Europe. (NARA)

Left: Senior Airman William Hynson signs the pre-flight forms for the 77th TFS F-111E for which he is Crew Chief, whilst deployed to Jever Air Base, West Germany, during 1985. (NARA)

A 79th TFS, 20th TFW, F-111E pilot (note his squadron-coloured scarf) looks towards other F-111Es during 1987. His helmet is the lightweight HGU-55/P, introduced in 1983 and which became standard during the 1980s. This illustrates the pilot's good view to the left in the F-111; however, the side-by-side seating meant that pilot visibility to the right was poor. For this reason F-111s generally flew in pairs, although four-ship formations were used by the 48th TFW F-111Fs for Operation El Dorado Canyon in 1986. (NARA)

As NATO's foremost striker, the F-111 would have been a primary tactical nuclear weapons deliverer. The B61 (0.3 to 340 kiloton yield) was the main such weapon available to the F-111. The B43 (70 kiloton to 1 megaton yield) was available until the mid-1980s and the B57 (5 to 20 kiloton yield) until the end of the decade. The B83 (1.2 megaton yield) entered service in the late 1980s, replacing the B43 amongst others. The introduction of GLCM and Pershing II later in the decade freed the F-111 fleet from some of their nuclear alert duties, allowing them to focus more on conventional operations. Like all nuclear-capable USAFE units, the F-111 wings maintained a 'Victor Alert': jets fully fuelled and armed with tactical nuclear bombs, on alert to launch at 15 minutes' notice. The normal tour for alert crews was two days during the week and three days on the weekend, with crew changeover on the mornings on Monday, Wednesday and Friday.

The F-111F model later added Precision Guided Munition (PGM) delivery capability. The AN/AVQ-26 Pave Tack laser designation pod, developed for carriage by the F-4E and RF-4C (the latter using it as a recon sensor), featured forward-looking infrared and was the first pod to allow night target designation. The bulky pod was nicknamed 'Pave Drag' by F-4 crews. Relatively few Phantoms were equipped with it, most of the 150 pods produced being transferred for use by F-111Fs, which could carry the pod internally in the weapons bay. Between 1981 and 1984 all USAFE F-111Fs were Pave Tack equipped, allowing autonomous designation for Laser Guided Bombs (LGBs). LGBs were the older Paveway II models (the 2,000 lb GBU-10, using either standard Mk 84 or BLU-109 penetrating warheads and the 500 lb GBU-12 with Mk 82 warhead) and the improved Paveway III (2,000 lb GBU-24 with Mk 84 or BLU-109 warheads). The more efficient Paveway III featured increased range and accuracy, better suited to low-level employment, also being known as Low-Level LGBs (LLLGBs). Another alternative PGM was the GBU-15 glide bomb, hitting targets with precision after gliding some distance. Pave Tack was not used with GBU-15, AXQ-14 or ZSW-1 datalink pods being required instead, carried on the under-fuselage aft ECM pod station (displacing the ECM pod to the forward station). The expensive GBU-15 was considered a silver bullet, reserved for high-priority, well-defended targets. Consequently, only one F-111F squadron (493rd TFS) was so equipped.

The 20th Tactical Fighter Wing (TFW), with 'UH' tail code, operated the F-111E from RAF Upper Heyford from 1970. Its components were the 55th Tactical Fighter Squadron (55th TFS) 'Fightin' 55th' (its aircraft having a blue or blue/white check fin stripe), 77th TFS 'Gamblers' (red fin stripe) and 79th TFS 'Tigers' (yellow or tiger-stripe fin stripe). The wing initially received seventy-nine F-111Es, dropping to seventy-six by 1989.

Seen over the northern English Channel during 1987, 77th and 79th TFS F-111Es and a 42nd ECS EF-111A take turns refuelling from a Utah ANG (191st AREFS, 151st AREFG) KC-135E on TDY with the ETTF. (NARA)

A pair of 79th TFS F-111Es head to the bombing range at RAF Tain, northern Scotland, during 1987. They carry live Mk 82 AIR bombs outboard and SUU-21 practice bomb dispensers inboard. (NARA)

A 493rd TFS, 48th TFW, F-111F seen in 1982. Its underside Pave Tack pod head is pointing directly at the camera and it is carrying GBU-10 Paveway II LGBs with Mk 84 2,000 lb warheads. (NARA)

Another 493rd TFS F-111F, seen taking off from Hahn Air Base in West Germany during exercise Reforger '86, showing off its sturdy undercarriage. (NARA)

The 493rd TFS was the only USAFE unit equipped with the GBU-15 glide bomb. Available with EO (electro-optical, i.e. daylight) or infra-red homing heads and with Mk 84 2,000 lb HE or BLU-109 2,000 lb penetrator warheads, a GBU-15(V)-1 with EO head and Mk 84 warhead is visible under the wing of this F-111F, viewed from a tanker in 1988. The opposite wing is balanced by two SUU-21 practice bomb dispensers. (NARA)

A pair of 495th TFS F-111Fs over the Mediterranean whilst operating from Morón Air Base, Spain, during exercise Open Gate '89. Both are carrying a pair of SUU-21 practice bomb dispensers inboard and a single CATM-9P (an AIM-9P training round) under the starboard outer wing. (NARA)

The F-111E (developed as an interim variant, due to technical delays with the digital avionics of the intended definitive model, the F-111D) featured simplified analogue avionics from the original F-111A. By the mid-1980s it was decided to upgrade the F-111E with digital avionics (under AMP, 'Avionics Modernization Program'); however, deliveries did not get underway until 31 January 1991.

On 1 July 1983 the 42nd Electronic Combat Squadron (ECS) 'NATO Ravens' activated under 20th TFW, equipped with the newly converted EF-111A Raven jets, building up to a fleet of seventeen aircraft. In 1985 the 42nd ECS was reassigned on paper to the 66th Electronic Combat Wing (ECW) at Sembach Air Base, West Germany; however, the 42nd ECS remained at Upper Heyford, attached to the 20th TFW, despite its administrative reassignment.

The Electronic Warfare (EW) EF-111A, modified from surplus F-111A airframes, integrated the AN/ALQ-99E radar jamming system, a repackaged version of the system used in US Navy (USN) EA-6Bs. The handful of EF-111As, known as 'Spark Varks', were key assets, as NATO's only supersonic stand-off or penetrating electronic jamming aircraft.

The F-111F equipped the 48th TFW 'Statue of Liberty' at RAF Lakenheath (tail code 'LN') with a total of ninety aircraft in 1980, dropping to eighty-one by 1989. Assigned squadrons were the 492nd TFS 'Bolars' (blue fin stripe), 493rd TFS 'Grim Reapers' (yellow fin stripe), 494th TFS 'Panthers' (red fin stripe) and the 495th TFS, which also acted as the training squadron (green fin stripe).

The F-111F was the ultimate model, using a modified form of the SAC FB-111A's Mk 2B digital avionics. It featured completely redesigned TF30-P-100 engines, resulting in improved performance and much increased thrust. An F-111F's total thrust was over 50,000 lb compared to 37,000 lb from the pair of TF-30-P-3s of F-111E/EF-111As.

Following the withdrawal of GLCMs from Europe, the USAF announced in July 1988 that fifty retiring SAC FB-111As would be converted for tactical duties as the F-111G and issued to a UK-based unit, although no details were given as to the unit or base. Although the conversions took place, the conclusion of the Cold War ensured they served with US-based units, never reaching USAFE.

An EF-111A Raven of the 42nd ECS. The squadron had just been reassigned to the 66th ECW at Sembach at the time of this June 1985 photograph; however, it remained attached to the 20th TFW at Upper Heyford. (NARA)

A 42nd ECS EF-111A approaches Gibraltar during exercise Open Gate '89. The regular exercise practiced keeping the Straits of Gibraltar open during wartime. (NARA)

A 495th TFS F-111F during Open Gate '89, alongside a KC-135E of the 126th AREFS, 128th AREFG, Wisconsin Air National Guard, which was supporting the exercise. (NARA)

A 495th TFS F-111F (carrying a CATM-9P and SUU-21s) refuels from another Wisconsin ANG KC-135E, this one wearing the dark 'KC-135 Aircraft Camouflage Pattern' (often nicknamed 'Shamu', after the killer whale, by crews) introduced in the late 1980s. (NARA)

A moody shot of a 495th TFS F-111F at Morón AB during Open Gate '89, carrying a CATM-9P and SUU-21s. A Wisconsin ANG KC-135E is visible in the rear. (NARA)

The other main 3 AF type was the A-10A Thunderbolt II. Unique as a highly survivable tank killing and CAS (close air support) type, the A-10A replaced the F-4D with the UK-based 81st TFW from 1978. Whilst most Air Force wings had three or four assigned squadrons, by 1 January 1980 the 81st TFW had built-up to six squadrons, based across the 'twin airfields' of RAF Bentwaters and RAF Woodbridge, 1.5 miles apart. The 81st TFW (tailcode 'WR') was at Bentwaters along with the assigned 92nd TFS 'Skulls' (or 'Avengers') (yellow fin stripe), 509th TFS 'Pirates' (grey fin stripe), 510th TFS 'Buzzards' (purple fin stripe) and 511th TFS 'Vultures' (black fin stripe). Meanwhile, the 78th TFS 'Bushmasters' (locally known as 'Snakes') (red fin stripe) and 91st TFS 'Blue Streaks' (blue fin stripe) were at RAF Woodbridge.

Unlike the F-111s, which would have fought the Third World War from their home bases, the 81st TFW would have deployed to West German Forward Operating Locations (FOLs) in wartime (whilst reinforcing fighter units from the US would have moved into Bentwaters/Woodbridge). These FOLs were not just in the southern (4 ATAF) area of West Germany (where USAFE units were based); half were in the northern (2 ATAF) area. Four of these FOL Dets were maintained in peacetime, with a further two to be added in wartime.

Det 1 was at Sembach AB (4 ATAF area, maintained by the 510th TFS until 1989, subsequently 78th TFS), Det 2 at Leipheim AB (4 ATAF, 92d TFS until 1989, then 91st TFS), Det 3 at Ahlhorn AB (2 ATAF, 91st TFS until 1989, then 509th TFS) and Det 4 at Nörvenich AB (2 ATAF, 78th TFS until 1989, then 510th TFS). The two additional wartime FOLs were at Jever AB (2 ATAF, 509th TFS until 1989, then 511th TFS) and Wiesbaden AB (4 ATAF, 511th TFS until 1989, then 92nd TFS).

The FOLs had permanent staff of about seventy-five personnel (including operations, maintenance, munitions, logistics, and communications specialists),

Above: An 81st TFW A-10A is refuelled on the ground at its RAF Bentwaters base during 1981. (NARA)

Right: An 81st TFW A-10A, viewed from a tanker over the North Sea during 1980, wearing the initial grey camouflage scheme. (NARA)

under the command of a USAF lieutenant colonel pilot. When the A-10 squadrons deployed forward they would bring their own personnel and integrate with the detachment staff to form a larger US squadron under the operational control of the host base's wing, under NATO command. For example, at Nörvenich, the 78th TFS would deploy forward, integrating with the US permanent party and aligning as a third squadron under the Luftwaffe's JBG 31 (31st Fighter-Bomber Wing), alongside the German wing's two Tornado IDS squadrons. At Leipheim the 92nd TFS would form a squadron under the Luftwaffe's CAS Alpha Jet-equipped JBG 44, and so on.

In peacetime the 81st TFW maintained thirty-two A-10As at the four peacetime FOLs (eight at each). Individual pilots would spend two weeks at the FOL, flying about twice a day, followed by four weeks back in the UK, flying about twice a week. In wartime the two additional FOLs would be activated, all six housing about eighteen A-10As. As well as these formal FOLs, in wartime 81st TFW A-10s could alternatively deploy elsewhere in northern or southern Europe supporting NATO's flanks.

In 1987 the 10th Tactical Reconnaissance Wing at RAF Alconbury (discussed below) was redesignated the 10th Tactical Fighter Wing, resulting in some reorganisation of the A-10 community. During 1987/88, the 10th TFW lost its RF-4C squadron and transferred its 527th Aggressor Squadron (q.v.) to the 81st TFW at Bentwaters. Meanwhile, the 81st TFW's 509th TFS and 511th TFS were reassigned to the 10th TFW at Alconbury, easing some of the crowding at their former base. The two squadrons took on the AR tailcode, but retained their former squadron colours. Meanwhile, the wartime FOL assignments of the squadrons remained as previously, until the 1989 switch-around of TFS-FOL assignments. Peacetime A-10 FOL deployments remained at thirty-two aircraft, 81st TFW commitments dropping to twenty-four, the remaining eight now coming from the 10th TFW. a total of 116 A-10As were operated by the 10th and 81st TFWs by 1989.

Also seen during 1981, this 81st TFW A-10A at Bentwaters sports the then relatively new 'European I' camouflage pattern, or 'Charcoal Lizard' scheme. Whilst the former grey scheme was effective when viewed against the sky from the ground, when viewed from the air by other aircraft the light grey scheme stood out against typical dark green European terrain. This increased its vulnerability to enemy fighters, resulting in this new scheme becoming standard. After the Cold War, however, A-10s reverted to a light grey scheme similar to the original scheme as they then faced a reduced air-to-air threat. This A-10 is being loaded with four TV-guided AGM-65A/B Mavericks, whilst the four on the trolley in the foreground await loading onto another A-10. (NARA)

Seen during exercise Certain Sentinel/Reforger '86, this 509th TFS, 81st TFW, A-10A sports the short-lived Battelle 'Tickler' – more formally known as the GFU-16/A Gun Gas Diverter – on the front of the gun barrel. Introduced to remedy the issue of the engines ingesting gun gasses when the latter is fired, causing flameouts, the diverter caused structural issues and was therefore removed from the few A-10s that had received them. Meanwhile, the problem was resolved by ammunition propellant mixture changes and modifying the engine ignition system to come on when the gun was fired. This aircraft also carries an ALQ-119 (long) ECM pod on the starboard outer pylon, whilst the pod on the fuselage-side pylon below the cockpit is an AN/AAS-35(V) Pave Penny laser spot tracker, allowing the aircraft to detect targets laser-designated by third parties. (NARA)

The A-10A itself was designed to survive having one engine, one tail section or a large wing section shot off and had triple-redundant flight controls featuring control cables (less susceptible to jamming if damaged) rather than rods. Intentionally slow (pilots joking that it was 'the only airplane vulnerable to rear hemisphere birdstrikes'), it was nicknamed Warthog due to its ungainly appearance. It was entirely designed around the massive GAU-8/A Avenger seven-barrelled 30 mm cannon, firing beer-bottle-sized depleted uranium shells, intended to be used primarily for anti-tank use. The standard 'combat mix' (CM) of ammunition for anti-armour use was a five-to-one mix of PGU-14/B Armor Piercing Incendiary (API) and PGU-13/B High Explosive Incendiary (HEI) rounds. Initially with a selectable rate of fire (2,100 or 4,200 rounds per minute), around 1987 this was fixed at 3,900 rounds per minute. As bursts are only of a few seconds, a more meaningful measure is sixty-five rounds per second, although only fifty rounds are fired in the first second whilst the gun spins up to speed. One early problem was gasses created when the gun was fired, causing engine flameouts, resulting in the last pre-production YA-10A crashing after suffering a double engine flameout during tests. Double engine failures are a particular problem for the A-10 as the maximum level speed of an A-10 is lower than the relight speed of the TF34 engines. If high enough an A-10 can dive to achieve relight speed, but at low levels the pilot had no option but to eject. After several failed 'cures' the gun gas ingestion problem was resolved by ammunition propellant mixture changes, plus making the engine ignition system come on when the gun fired, ensuring the engines keep running if gas is ingested.

It could tote a large load of other weapons on its eleven hardpoints, AGM-65 Maverick air-to-ground missiles (AGMs) being the primary anti-tank weapon. The original daytime-only AGM-65A and B models with TV seeker heads (the latter with scene magnification to lock on to targets from twice the range) were joined by D models with imaging intra-red (IIR) seeker from 1986. AGM-65G with IIR seeker and heavyweight penetrator warhead were entering service at the end of the 1980s. From 1986 A-10s would normally carry an equal mix of AGM-65B and D models. Cluster bombs were used for area targets, including the new CBU-87/89 models or the older Mk 20 Rockeye and SUU-30H dispenser family. Mk 82 iron bombs were also an option. Self-defence AIM-9L/Ms were carried as well as ECM pods – AN/ALQ-119 (long) being replaced by AN/ALQ-131 pods (both deep and shallow models) during the decade.

For their primary anti-armour role, A-10As would rely mainly on the AGM-65 and GAU-8/A, which were not only more effective than dumb and cluster bombs, but did not require direct overflight of the target like the latter. The cannon was generally fired from 2,500 feet away from the target until the aircraft was within 1,500 feet of the target. Mavericks were generally fired about 9 miles away from the target.

A-10s operated in pairs (or larger groups) at ultra-low-level, supporting each other. If enemy anti-aircraft vehicles were present and could be identified (for example by a forward air controller – FAC), it would be desirable to target those before moving on to the other enemy armour; however, in reality A-10 pilots would more likely hit targets as they saw them, not having the luxury of time to identify, never mind pick and choose, their targets.

If attacking area targets (maybe a column of soft-skin vehicles, or personnel in the open) with either iron or cluster bombs, one A-10 pilot conducted the bomb run, whilst his wingman would suppress the target with his gun: hitting the target from low down, approaching from a right angle to the axis of the other A-10 attack, fishtailing his rudders left and right, yawing gunfire along the length of the column.

A-10s were even more effective if they co-ordinated their efforts with attack helicopters. Exercises illustrated a reduced A-10/attack helicopter loss rate and an increased kill rate of enemy vehicles. Tactics known as the Joint Air Attack Team (JAAT), would have seen A-10s working with US Army helicopters and artillery. Perhaps working the flank of a WarPac armoured penetration, artillery would be used to keep enemy armour crews buttoned up, preventing defensive use of their roof-mounted heavy machine guns, whilst the helicopters could pop up from behind cover and prioritise hitting the anti-aircraft vehicles. As the helicopters moved off using 'nap of the earth' flight to another firing position, the A-10s would pop up from behind terrain and hit the armour before dropping behind cover once again, upon which the helicopters would pop up from their new positions and fire more missiles at the armour, and so on.

The USAF leadership periodically tried to kill off the A-10, being unenthusiastic about the CAS mission, preferring to fight their own war rather than support the Army. This USAF outlook was deeply at odds with the highly co-ordinated joint approach to warfare that was the new reality from 1982 onwards, known as the 'AirLand Battle' concept. However, this new concept presented a new threat to the A-10 as it focussed on exploiting US technological advantages, especially night fighting, where US forces had an advantage. Furthermore, the importance of striking follow-on forces deeper behind the front line, isolating front line enemy forces from reinforcements, was also stressed. The A-10 was largely a fair weather, daytime-only jet. In Europe that meant there would be extended periods where conditions would be too marginal for it to fly even in the day, never mind at night. It was also slow and relatively vulnerable to enemy fighters if deep in the enemy rear. The USAF's new Close Air Support/Battlefield Air Interdiction (CAS/BAI) requirement led to intentions to relegate the A-10 to the 'Fast FAC' role (replacing the OA-37B and OV-10A) and use a night/adverse weather capable, CAS configured version of the F-16, plus rebuilt supersonic night/adverse

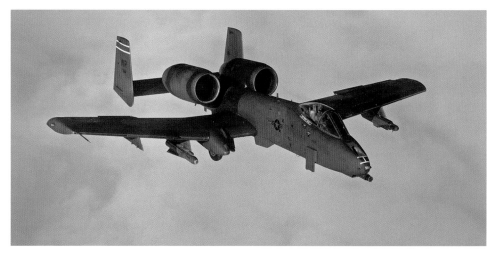

Seen over the North Sea during 1988, this 78th TFS, 81st TFW, A-10A from RAF Woodbridge carries a Maverick training round under the starboard wing and an ALQ-131 (shallow) ECM pod to port. (NARA)

weather versions of the A-7D (the A-7F), to take on the CAS/BAI role. Small numbers of US-based A-10s started to be re-roled for FAC (redesignated OA-10A despite being unmodified) from 1987 and New York Air National Guard F-16As got a 30 mm podded gun (GPU-5). However, 3 AF's A-10 fleet was not replaced and they saw out the remainder of the Cold War; the supposed replacements did not come to fruition, the A-10 being reprieved, going on to serve with distinction over the battlefield for many more decades.

The 10th Tactical Reconnaissance Wing (TRW) at RAF Alconbury controlled the 1st Tactical Reconnaissance Squadron (TRS) – 'AR' tailcode / blue squadron fin stripe – operating twenty-three RF-4C recon jets as of 1980, at least some of which were Pave Tack compatible (used for stand-off infra-red recon of targets too hot to overfly, rather than for target designation). Also assigned to the wing was the 527th Tactical Fighter Training Aggressor Squadron with the F-5E.

The 1st TRS ceased operations on 1 July 1987 and transferred its RF-4Cs to other units. The squadron had been one of only two RF-4C units in USAFE for several years after the slow drawdown of Europe-based RF-4C units started in the late 1970s (the 10th TRW's two other RF-4C squadrons inactivating in 1976, and Germany-based 26th TRW going down to one TRS from two in 1978). The USAF was going in a different direction with tactical recon, literally: upwards. Although RF-4Cs would survive in USAF service into the 1990s, throughout the 1980s the USAF slowly moved away from tactical recon fast jets, penetrating at low level, with the introduction of SAC's Europe-based high-level TR-1A (new build, tactical recon focused U-2R variants).

An RF-4C of the 1st TRS, 10th TRW, flies over its base at RAF Alconbury, England. Note the AN/AVQ-26 Pave Tack pod on the underside centreline, plus an ALQ-131 (deep) ECM pod under the starboard wing. In this 1983 shot, the aircraft is seen still wearing the Vietnam-era 'South East Asia' ('SEA') camouflage scheme with three-colour upper sides (tan, dark green and medium green) and light grey undersides. (NARA)

Seen in early 1987, just months before the unit disbanded, this 1st TRS, 10th TRW, RF-4C in wing commander's markings is in the 'European I' camouflage scheme that was introduced during the 1980s. This was a 'wraparound' scheme (i.e. lacking the light grey undersides of the 'SEA' scheme) and retained the dark green and medium green used in the 'SEA' scheme but replaced the former tan with dark grey. (NARA)

As outlined above, the 10th TRW became the 10th TFW on 20 August 1987 and the A-10A equipped 509th and 511th TFS transferred in from the 81st TFW (on 1 June and 1 September 1988 respectively).

The 527th Tactical Fighter Training Aggressor Squadron was USAFE's sole Aggressor unit. Activated in 1976 under the 10th TRW, it received twenty F-5E aggressor jets during May/June of that year. By 1980 it held eighteen F-5Es. Redesignated the 527th Aggressor Squadron on 15 April 1983, their F-5Es wore typically colourful aggressor markings. The 527th hosted USAFE units, providing Dissimilar Air Combat Training (DACT), and also hit the road, visiting USAFE and other NATO units throughout Europe to hone their air combat skills. They also formed a key part of the 'red air' in exercises, for example exercise Red Star '87, which trained USAFE F-15C crews in countering WarPac tactics, with 'red air' formations of USAFE F-111s (simulating Soviet interdictors) escorted by 527th AS F-5Es (simulating the escorting Soviet fighters). The 527th also maintained a semi-regular det of six jets at Decimomannu Air Base ('Deci') in Sardinia, home to Europe's only Air Combat Manoeuvring Instrumentation (ACMI) range at that time.

In wartime the 527th AS had an air defence role and would have been integrated into 11 Group of the Royal Air Force, responsible for the UK Air Defence Region. Consequently, each year the 527th took part in at least one of the twice-yearly internal 11 Group exercise 'Priory' air defence drills (renamed exercise 'Elder Joust' from April 1987). Whilst F-5Es could carry training versions of the AIM-9L, they could not fire live versions. Consequently, for the wartime role, the 527th's F-5Es would have carried earlier AIM-9P-3/4s. A former 527th pilot recounted to the author how, during an early 1980s UK air show, a well-informed Prince Charles visiting their display aircraft asked why they did not have more effective AIM-9Ls for their wartime role.

Fatigue problems with some of their F-5E fleet resulted in operating (g-force) limitations; meanwhile, the arrival of new Soviet fighter threats like the MiG-29, which the F-5E could not adequately simulate, led to the decision to upgrade to the F-16C, coinciding with the unit moving to RAF Bentwaters and reassignment to the 81st TFW. Of the, by now, nineteen-strong F-5E fleet, the seven jets with the least hours were transferred to the USN for further use as USN Adversaries, whilst the remaining twelve,

This trio of 527th Tactical Fighter Training Aggressor Squadron F-5Es are seen on 15 January 1983, exactly three months before the unit was redesignated the 527th Aggressor Squadron. They display the diverse aggressor schemes worn by the unit, and each aircraft carries a pair of inert CATM-9Es (captive training versions of the AIM-9E Sidewinder). (NARA)

This pair of 527th AS F-5Es carry CATM-9Ps (captive training versions of the AIM-9P Sidewinder) and wear a grey camouflage scheme. They are seen heading out towards the English Channel for DACT training during 1987. (NARA)

These CATM-9P-carrying 527th AS F-5Es are seen at RAF Alconbury during exercise Red Star '87. The 527th AS hosted the exercise each year, and saw F-5E aggressors and USAFE F-111s simulate Soviet packages (the F-111s simulating strikers such as Su-24s and the F-5Es simulating their MiG-23/29/Su-27 escorts) to train USAFE F-15C/D units. Bitburg-based F-15C/Ds of the 22nd TFS, 36th TFW, took part in the 1987 exercise. (NARA)

Left: Pilots and crews from the F-15C/D-equipped 22nd TFS and F-5E-equipped 527th AS during briefing for a mission during exercise Red Star '87 in the latter unit's briefing room at RAF Alconbury. (NARA)

Below: This 527th AS F-5E is seen deployed to 'Deci' (Decimomannu Air Base in Sardinia) to use the nearby Air Combat Manoeuvring Instrumentation (ACMI) range. Seen in the background are F-15C Eagles of the 22nd TFS, 36th TFW, from Bitburg AB, West Germany. This January 1988 scene is just six months before the 527th traded in its F-5Es for F-16Cs and moved from RAF Alconbury to join the 81st TFW at RAF Bentwaters. (NARA)

which had cracked longerons behind the canopy sill, were transferred to US allies including Morocco and Tunisia after repair at the RAF Kemble depot. On 14 July 1988 the 527th AS set up with the F-16C Block 30 at RAF Bentwaters as part of the 81st TFW, initially receiving two aircraft, one each from 52nd and 86th TFW in Germany, slowly building up to twelve aircraft (of an intended eighteen). By November pilot conversion was complete, and the 527th hosted six 36th TFW F-15Cs for a three-week DACT course. The 527th's F-16Cs never received the usual exotic aggressor schemes, merely having large Soviet-style red 'Bort numbers' added to the usual paint scheme, along with a red fin stripe and 'WR' tail code. This existence was short-lived; the abrupt end of the Cold War resulting in the 527th winding down operations and passing its aircraft to other units from November 1989, inactivating on 30 September 1990.

Introduced in the 1980s, the Ground Launched Cruise Missile – GLCM (pronounced 'glick-um') – was a class of weapon not in the arsenal since the withdrawal of Matador and Mace in the 1960s. The emergence of a new generation of Soviet intermediate range nuclear weapons represented a grave new threat to NATO, particularly feared by NATO's European members as it exclusively targeted Western Europe. Particularly concerning was the RSD-10 Pioneer (SS-20 Saber) intermediate range ballistic missile. Mobile, and concealable, on its transporter erector launcher (TEL), each 3,000-mile range SS-20 was armed with three 150 kt independently targetable warheads. The US-Soviet SALT Treaty of 1972 had brought parity to strategic, but not tactical, nuclear weapons and Western suspicions were that the Soviets were seeking a nuclear weapons advantage in the European theatre. It seems in hindsight that Soviet aims were to drive the West to make further arms concessions. If so, this backfired, as in response the US decided in 1979 to develop and deploy to Europe both the US Army Pershing II missile and the USAF GLCM. The GLCM was a mobile, ground-launched, nuclear-armed (W84 thermonuclear warhead with a 0.2–150 kt variable-yield) 1,600-mile (2,500 kilometre) range weapon based on the USN's Tomahawk cruise missile. During the development and early stages of deployment of these weapons, US/Soviet negotiations to outlaw intermediate nuclear weapons were held, although they were not productive and by 1983 the West German Bundestag voted to accept the deployment of US missiles, the Soviets then pulling out of the talks. The US deployment continued. Plans were ultimately for six bases across Europe (two in the UK and single sites in Belgium, Italy, the Netherlands and West Germany) to house the missiles. The first operational unit, the 501st Tactical Missile Wing at RAF Greenham Common, activated on 1 July 1982 and the wing's 11th Tactical Missile Squadron (activated 1 October 1982) was assigned ninety-six GLCMs. The second UK-based 3 AF wing, 303rd TMW and its 87th TMS, activated 12 December 1986 at RAF Molesworth; assigned sixty-four GLCMs, it only received sixteen before deliveries were frozen due to the INF Treaty.

Tactical Missile Squadrons were organised into flights with sixteen GLCMs (four TEL vehicles, each carrying four GLCMs, plus two truck-mounted 'Launch Control Centers' – LCC). Each flight of four TELs and two LCCs was housed in a specially constructed hardened Ready Storage Shelter (RSS), clusters of which, along with other support buildings, were within the high security GLCM Alert and Maintenance Area (GAMA) within their assigned base. In times of tension the flights would leave their bases, dispersing to distant pre-surveyed locations, making them difficult for the Soviets to target.

Powered by a small F107 turbofan, the subsonic GLCMs would take around two and a half hours from launch to reach targets at extreme range. However, they flew very low using Terrain Contour Matching (TERCOM) and were almost undetectable.

Left: A test launch of a BGM-109G
GLCM from its Transporter-Erector-
Launcher (TEL) at the Utah Test and
Training Range during 1982. (NARA)

Below: The high security GLCM Alert
and Maintenance Area (GAMA) for
the ninety-six BGM-109G GLCMs of
the 501st Tactical Missile Wing at RAF
Greenham Common. Each of the six
Ready Storage Shelters housed a Flight
of four Transporter-Erector-Launcher
vehicles (each carrying four GLCMs)
and two Launch Control Center (LCC)
vehicles. In times of tension the Flights
would leave their bases to disperse to
distant pre-surveyed locations, making
them difficult for the Soviets to target.
(NARA)

The Army's Pershing II missiles reached their targets up to 1,100 miles (1,770 km) away in just 10 to 15 minutes – if detected, they were too fast to be stoppable.

The Soviets were fearful of the combined threat these missiles posed and made it a priority to inhibit their deployment. It remains unclear how much credit could be given to Soviet propaganda, fed into the West via the KGB, for the development of the small, but vocal, anti-cruise missile movement that developed in Western Europe in the 1980s. It is notable however that the focus of the protests was purely on US cruise missiles, rather than the Soviet SS-20s that were already in place and targeting the West. Perhaps the most famous of the anti-cruise movements was the 'Greenham Common Women's Peace Camp', causing occasional security concerns and complications for the 501st TMW. However, these peace movements failed to inhibit the deployment of GLCMs and the Soviets came back to the negotiating table. President Reagan and Soviet General Secretary Gorbachev signed the Intermediate-Range Nuclear Forces (INF) Treaty on 8 December 1987 and it was ratified on 1 June 1988. The INF Treaty banned both nations' land-based ballistic and cruise missiles (and missile launchers), both short/medium (310–620 mile/500–1,000 km) and intermediate (620–3,420 mile/1,000–5,500 km) range.

As a result GLCMs, and other banned weapons held by both sides, started to be withdrawn and destroyed, both parties sending inspectors to observe and verify the destruction. The 303rd TMW/ 87th TMS at RAF Molesworth inactivated on 31 January 1989. The 501st TMW/ 11th TMS at RAF Greenham Common, which had been Europe's first operational GLCM unit, also became its last when it inactivated on 31 May 1991.

The 513th Tactical Airlift Wing (TAW), the host wing at RAF Mildenhall, controlled the 10th Airborne Command and Control Squadron (ACCS) with its four EC-135H 'Silk Purse' airborne command post aircraft. The 10th ACCS maintained one EC-135H on 24-hour ground alert at Mildenhall, and (from summer 1984 onwards) another detached aircraft on 24-hour ground alert at Lajes Field in the Azores. The EC-135H carried a battle staff headed by a general or flag officer, designated the Airborne Emergency Action Officer (AEAO), ready to assume interim authority if their ground-based opposite numbers were made inoperative or destroyed. The wing was redesignated 513th Airborne Command and Control Wing on 18 June 1987. Late in the decade a single WC-135B was added as a trainer and support aircraft.

An EC-135H of the 10th ACCS, 513th TAW, seen over its base at RAF Mildenhall during 1983. A C-5 Galaxy and a C-12 can be seen on the ground below. (NARA)

Finally, Third Air Force also controlled two non-flying Air Base Groups (ABGs). The 7020th ABG at RAF Fairford provided support for SAC's 11th Strategic Group. The 7274th ABG at RAF Chicksands provided support to the 693d Electronic Security Wing of Electronic Security Command's 'European Electronic Security Division'.

Sixteenth Air Force

Despite covering the greatest geographic area of USAFE's Air Forces, with bases from Spain to Turkey, Sixteenth Air Force (16 AF), HQ Torrejón Air Base (AB), Spain, had the least assets: a single wing, the 401st TFW at Torrejón AB, Spain. With the 'TJ' tail code, its squadrons were 612th TFS 'Fightin' Eagles', 613th TFS 'Squids' and 614th TFS 'Lucky Devils', also maintaining Detachment 2 at Morón Air Base, Spain. The wing upgraded from the F-4C to the F-4D in 1978/79 and to F-16A/B Block 15s during 1983, the first five aircraft arriving with the 612th TFS on 19 March,

A pair of F-16A Block 15s of the 614th TFS, 401st TFW. Each jet carries a white SUU-20 practice bomb dispenser. The SUU-20 could hold six practice bombs or four 2.74-inch rockets (although the latter were rarely used in SUU-20s). The practice bombs were carried exposed on the underside of the dispenser and were explosively ejected. A single 300 US Gal. fuel tank is in the centreline of both aircraft. (NARA)

The same pair of 614th TFS, 401st TFW, F-16A Block 15s seen in the previous photograph, on approach to Torrejón Air Base, during 1985. (NARA)

marred by the last aircraft accidentally landing wheels-up, causing minor damage, then being dropped by a crane during recovery, causing major damage. In 1988 the wing converted to the F-16C/D Block 30 (featuring the new, more powerful, alternate F-16 engine – the General Electric F110-GE-100 – instead of Pratt & Whitney F-100 variants of previous F-16s), holding sixty-seven and four respectively by 1989. Whilst the 401st had a nuclear mission and performed local air defence, its primary role was conventional air-to-ground. There were no nuclear weapons located at Torrejón AB, but 401st TFW maintained aircraft on nuclear 'Victor Alert' elsewhere; at all times three jets were with the 39th Tactical Group (TG) at Incirlik AB, Turkey, armed with B61 tactical nuclear bombs (weapons hosted at that base), a similar alert being maintained with the 40th TG at Aviano AB, Italy. Wartime contingencies would have seen more wing aircraft operating with those from Incirlik and Aviano.

Unusually, the squadrons of the 401st regularly changed their squadron fin colour. The 612th alternated between solid blue fin stripes and blue/white checkerboard, settling on the latter by the F-16 period. The 613th had yellow with black stars, changing from stars to lightning flashes before settling on a yellow/black checkerboard on the F-16. The 614th had red with black diamonds, and solid black before moving to a red/black checkerboard by the time of the F-16. At one point in the F-4 days, all three squadrons used a black/white checkerboard.

The US presence in Spain was unpopular; consequently in 1988 the US and Spain agreed to the withdrawal of the 401st TFW and most US forces from Spain by 1991. This wind-down was delayed by the Gulf War, in which the 401st took part, but the final squadron – the 614th – inactivated on 1 January 1992. The, now, 401st Fighter Wing transferred on paper to Aviano AB without personnel or equipment, assuming the personnel and mission (supporting rotational units) of the 40th Tactical Support Wing (the former 40th Tactical Group – q.v.).

A 613th TFS F-16A Block 15 moves to the pre-contact position behind a tanker (note the open refuelling receptacle door on the spine) over Sicily in 1987. It carries a deep ALQ-131 pod under the fuselage, as well as SUU-20s and a CATM-9L (AIM-9L Sidewinder captive training round) on the port wingtip. On the starboard wingtip is an Acceleration Monitor Assembly (AMA) pod, which is a radar reflector used for training purposes. Finally, it has 370 US Gal. fuel tanks inboard underwing. (NARA)

A group of 613th TFS F-16As take turns to refuel from a 319th BMW KC-135A serving with the ETTF. They are seen deploying to Incirlik Air Base in Turkey during 1987. (NARA)

The F-16A Block 15s arrive for the 'break' over Incirlik. All aircraft carry centreline deep ALQ-131 ECM pods, 370 US Gal. underwing fuel tanks, SUU-21 practice bomb dispensers, CATM-9Ls to port (barely visible, apart from on the furthest jet) and AMA pods on the starboard wingtip. (NARA)

The 406th Tactical Fighter Training Wing (TFTW) at Zaragoza Air Base (AB), Spain, had no aircraft assigned, instead supporting USAFE squadrons deploying to Zaragoza to train at the Bardenas Reales Air-to-Ground Range.

In 1969 USAFE lost its primary air-to-ground bombing and gunnery range at El Uotia, in the Kingdom of Libya, 80 miles south-west of Wheelus AB, to which USAFE aircraft using the range deployed, following the Gaddafi-led coup.

The next-best option was the Spanish Air Force range at Bardenas Reales, in the north-eastern semi-desert, 35 miles north-west of Zaragoza. Whilst smaller than, and not having such good weather as, El Uotia, Bardenas was larger and enjoyed better weather than other ranges elsewhere in Europe. Agreement was reached with Spain, and the range was considerably improved (via US funding and Spanish manpower): targets were remodelled, strafing pits added, staff accommodation buildings built and range towers added. USAFE aircraft using the Bardenas Reales Air-to-Ground Range deployed to Zaragoza AB. USAFE training required the ability for pilots to progress from 25 lb practice bombs, then 500 lb inert bombs through to dropping 500 lb live bombs. However, initially, the Spanish would only allow USAFE to drop 25 lb practice bombs, whilst allowing Spanish Air Force jets to use live ordnance, despite USAFE being the primary user of the range. Inert bombs were finally allowed in the 1980s. The Spanish also required USAFE to cease operations for two weeks per year to allow farmers in surrounding areas to gather their harvest!

Targets constructed at Bardenas included an 'airfield' (complete with ex-Spanish F-86 targets), 'SAM sites', 'convoys' and 'bridges'.

An F-16A Block 15 of the 313th TFS, 50th TFW, drops a pair of inert Mk 84 2,000 lb practice bombs over the Bardenas Reales Air-to-Ground Range in Spain during 1986. Aircraft using the range deployed to nearby Zaragoza Air Base. (NARA)

Another F-16A Block 15 of the 313th TFS, 50th TFW, drops a BDU-38 practice bomb (the inert practice version of the B61 thermonuclear bomb) over Bardenas Reales during 1986. The 313rd TFS had just changed from white tail stripes to the orange seen here. (NARA)

The death of Spanish dictator General Francisco Franco in 1975 brought instability, and uncertainty for USAFE in Spain, as the country moved from dictatorship to democracy (and NATO membership in 1982). F-5Es of the 527th TFTAS started deploying to Zaragoza from 1976, flying sorties against units using the range, increasing training realism. The USAFE Tactics School was formed at Zaragoza, running a graduate course that included large strike packages and aggressors. The 406th TFTW also had access to the El Bergantine Range (a group of uninhabited islands off Spain's Mediterranean coast), where live bombs and LGBs could be used. The quality of the training was improving; meanwhile, usage of the range increased during the late 1970s, although a tightening of defence budgets then saw a reduction in usage.

US-Spanish relations hit a new low in 1983 with the introduction of GLCM and Pershing to Europe (although none were coming to Spain), plus Spanish disquiet regarding increased US involvement in their former colony of Nicaragua. Rising defence budgets of the 1980s soon saw Bardenas increasing its usage once again and facilities being further improved, with targets representing an 'industrial centre' and 'command and control centre' added, as well as ex-French M47 tank targets. Also added was an EW threat emitter and a radar transmitter to act as a target for F-4G Wild Weasels. Tactical strafe targets for A-10As and a digital scoring system were added.

The 406th TFTW presence in Spain and activities at Zaragoza and Bardenas ended with the general withdrawal of US forces from Spain during the early 1990s.

Sixteenth AF only boasted a single BGM-109G Gryphon GLCM wing; however, it was USAFE's largest and one of only two to receive its full missile complement.

First Lieutenant Steve Talley, left, of the 313th TFS and Captain Alan Gardner, right, of the 81st TFS, acting as safety observers during bombing practice in one of the towers at the Bardenas Reales bombing range in 1986. Spanish personnel are visible in the background. (NARA)

A 494th TFS, 48th TFW, F-111F drops its load of inert Mk 82 AIR bombs over Bardenas Reales in 1986. The 'ballute' retarders can be seen inflating and the Pave Tack can be seen tracking the target. Although Pave Tack was primarily intended for designating targets for laser-guided bombs, it would still be used when dropping dumb bombs, in which case its laser would be used as a rangefinder to improve bombing accuracy. The head would swivel to keep the target in sight after weapons release and observe the bombs impacting behind the aircraft, providing instant BDA (Bomb Damage Assessment). (NARA)

An F-4E of the 81st TFS, 52nd TFW, drops its load of eighteen inert Mk 82 500 lb bombs over Bardenas Reales during 1986. (NARA)

An F-16C Block 25 of the 10th TFS, 50th TFW, an A-10A of the 511th TFS, 81st TFW, and an F-15C of the 53rd TFS, 36th TFW, in flight whilst operating from Zaragoza during 1987. (NARA)

The 487th TMW activated at newly rebuilt Comiso Air Base, Sicily, Italy, on 30 June 1983, its component 302nd TMS activating 1 July 1983, receiving 112 GLCMs. The wing inactivated on 27 May 1991, complying with INF.

The 40th TG at Aviano AB, Italy, supported squadrons deploying to Aviano, including those training at the Maniago Air-to-Ground Range.

Italy was also the home to two Munitions Support Squadrons, which stored and maintained tactical nuclear weapons for wartime use by Italian Air Force units through NATO: the 7401st MSS at Rimini AB for use by 5° Stormo F-104S, later F-104S (ASA), jets and 7402nd MSS at Ghedi AB for use by 6° Stormo F-104Gs, later replaced by Tornado IDS.

Other notable units in Italy were the 7275th ABG (San Vito dei Normanni Air Station), providing logistic and administrative support to 6917th Electronic Security Group of Electronic Security Command. Finally, the 7555th Tactical Training Squadron at Decimomannu Air Base, Sardinia, supported squadrons training over the ACMI range west of Sardinia. 'Deci' (jointly operated by Italy, West Germany, the UK and the US) was Europe's only such facility.

TUSLOG ('The United States Logistics Group') headquartered at Ankara Air Station (AS), Turkey, served as the primary 16 AF command element in Turkey, commanding various USAFE units and supporting all other US military organisations and government agencies in Turkey. Notable USAFE TUSLOG elements included the 39th Tactical Group (designated 'TUSLOG Detachment 10' until 1 October 1982) at Incirlik AB, which provided logistical support to US units in southern and eastern Turkey, support for units deployed to the base (including Victor Alert F-4s/F-16s from the 401st TFW) and training for air crews using the Konya bombing range, 185 miles north-west of Incirlik. In November 1982 HQ USAFE separated the staff agencies of HQ TUSLOG with local responsibilities (becoming the 7217th ABG at Ankara AS) whilst those handling matters throughout Turkey retained the HQ TUSLOG title. The 7241st ABG, at Izmir AS, supported the two NATO headquarters LANDSOUTHEAST and 6 ATAF. The 7022nd Air Base Squadron at Pirinçlik Air Station supported the 19th Surveillance Squadron of SAC (q.v.).

TUSLOG also oversaw four Munitions Support Squadrons, holding tactical nuclear weapons for wartime use by Turkish Air Force units through NATO: the 7391st MSS (Balıkesir AB) for use by 9ci Ana Jet Us (AJU 9) F-104Gs, the 7392nd MSS (Eskişehir AB) for use by AJU 1 F-4Es, the 7393rd MSS (Mürted AB) for use by AJU 4 F-104Gs, later F-16Cs, and the 7394th MSS (Erhaç AB) for use by AJU 7 F-4Es.

In Greece, the 7206th ABG oversaw operations at Hellenikon AB (no flying units permanently assigned), whilst the 7276th ABG oversaw operations at the (non-flying facility) Iraklion Air Station, Crete, supporting the 6931st Electronic Security Squadron (SIGINT unit). The 7061st MSS at Araxos AB held tactical nuclear weapons for wartime use through NATO by Hellenic Air Force 116 Pterix F-104Gs.

Seventeenth Air Force

On the very front lines of the Cold War was Seventeenth Air Force (17 AF), headquartered at Sembach AB. US Forces in West Germany were concentrated in the south, a consequence of the German sector assigned to US forces after the Second World War.

The only 17 AF flying unit based outside West Germany was the 32nd TFS 'Wolfhounds' at Soesterberg AB, in the Netherlands ('CR' tail code, orange fin stripe colour outlined in green). Reporting directly to 17 AF rather than a wing, and – uniquely – under direct Dutch operational control, the squadron had an air defence mission supporting Royal Netherlands Air Force units. Transitioning from F-4Es to F-15A/Bs from December 1978 and to F-15C/Ds from June 1980, the unit held twenty-three F-15Cs and three Ds in 1989. The 32nd Tactical Fighter Group was activated on 16 November 1989 to control 32nd TFS and a number of non-flying support units.

On 4 July 1989 a Soviet MiG-23MLD 'Flogger-K' of the 871st IAP suffered engine trouble immediately after taking off from its base at Kołobrzeg, Poland. The pilot ejected, but the aircraft stabilised under autopilot and flew off westward, unmanned, crossing East Germany and penetrating NATO airspace into West Germany. The MiG was intercepted by 32nd TFS F-15Cs, the pilots noting it was unmanned. Escorting the errant jet across the Netherlands and Belgium the F-15s were ordered to shoot it down when it crossed the North Sea coast; however, the MiG started to veer left and headed instead for the French border. Running out of fuel, it crashed on the Belgian side of the border at Kortrijk, hitting a house and tragically killing a teenage occupant (the Soviet unit moved base to Brezg in Poland and changed its tactical codes from blue to yellow in the wake of the incident in a bid to hide the unit's identity).

A pair of Royal Netherlands Air Force controllers in the tower at Soesterberg Air Base whilst a 32nd TFS F-15A taxis out in the background during early 1980. A few months later the unit would transition from the F-15A/B to the F-15C/D. (NARA)

A 32d TFS F-15C having launched with live weapons from Zulu Alert during 1987. (NARA)

The same 32nd TFS F-15C seen in the previous photograph shows off its war load of live AIM-9L/M Sidewinder and AIM-7M Sparrow AAMs. (NARA)

The remainder of USAFE's F-15 fleet could be found in West Germany with the 36th TFW at Bitburg AB (tailcode 'BT'), undoubtedly the command's premier fighter wing. Assigned the 22nd TFS 'Stingers' (red fin stripe), 53rd TFS 'Tigers' (yellow fin stripe with black tiger stripes) and the 525th TFS 'Bulldogs' (blue fin stripe), the wing had converted from the F-4E to the F-15A/B in 1977 and quickly upgraded to the F-15C/D during 1980. As of 1989 the wing held seventy-four C models and six Ds. The F-15 units were USAFE's only purely air-to-air fighter units, and they would have likely been the first into action if the Cold War had turned hot, flying air defence, plus escort and air superiority missions. As well as carrying the almost standard USAF M61A1 Vulcan 20 mm internal cannon, the F-15s would have carried four AIM-9L/M Sidewinder short-range infra-red AAMs and four medium-range AIM-7F/M Sparrow AAMs. However, questions remained about the rules of engagement (ROE) in wartime; the crowded skies possibly dictated the visual identification (VID) of targets, precluding medium range AAM use. Furthermore, doubts remained about the effectiveness of the AIM-7, which required the launching aircraft to maintain radar contact with (and therefore fly towards) the target, to guide the Sparrow until impact. The famous 1970s Aimval/Aceval tests illustrated the problem. One engagement saw four F-15s engaging four F-5s with simulated AIM-7s. Whilst simulated AIM-7s were still 'in flight' towards them, the F-5s were able to 'launch' simulated AIM-9s back at the F-15s, all jets mutually 'destroying' each other; not the best approach for a war of attrition with numerous WarPac forces. This resulted in the development of the 'fire-and-forget' AIM-120 AMRAAM (Advanced Medium Range AAM). However, its protracted development meant that the AIM-7 would see out the remainder of the Cold War. Therefore, it is possible short-range AIM-9L/Ms may have been the F-15's primary weapon against WarPac fighters on the Central Front. One former Eagle pilot told the author, 'We practiced VID ROE every mission when training in Eagles [during the] early 80s ... we figured BVR [Beyond Visual Range] authority would be an unexpected and unlikely treat.' F-15s (and other NATO fighters) would have taken advantage of the 'God's-eye-view' of the air battle provided by the fleet of E-3 Sentry AWACS (Airborne Warning and Control System) operated jointly by NATO (whose eighteen aircraft may have been augmented by further USAF aircraft in wartime). E-3s would have managed the air battle from the rear, detecting low-flying enemy aircraft, guiding friendly fighters to intercept them and routing friendly strike aircraft around enemy interceptors. E-3s fed into the integrated NATO Air Defence Ground Environment (NADGE) and could fill gaps in the radar coverage caused by destruction of friendly radar sites. The equivalent Soviet A-50 'Mainstay' (replacing the less effective Tu-126 'Moss') did not enter service until 1985 and then only in small numbers. Therefore, NATO enjoyed a distinct advantage in this regard.

The West German Luftwaffe's two wings of F-4F interceptors only had a wartime interceptor role, being constrained by the 1945 agreements between the Soviets and the Western Allies. In peacetime, only RAF and USAF jets could police West German airspace (France not exercising its similar rights and obligations since 1966). Consequently, the peacetime air defence of northern West Germany fell to two squadrons of RAF Phantom FGR.2s at RAF Wildenrath, supported by the 32nd TFS F-15s at Soesterberg (also covering the Netherlands). Southern West Germany was covered by the F-15s of the 36th TFW at Bitburg and the F-4Es, later F-16C/Ds, of the 86th TFW at Ramstein (q.v.). These three US air bases therefore maintained a 24 hours a day, 365 days a year 'Zulu Alert', with fully fuelled and armed jets (four at Bitburg, two each at Soesterberg and Ramstein) in special

A pair of 53rd TFS, 36th TFW, F-15Cs about to take off whilst deployed to Bodø Air Base, Norway, during exercise Alloy Express in 1982. (NARA)

Seen on the flight line during 1987, in front of the Zulu Alert facility at Bitburg Air Base, are 525th TFS, 36th TFW, F-15Cs. (NARA)

'barns' near the runway end. Pilots took it in turns to spend 24 hours – fully dressed in flight gear – ready to launch with 5 minutes' notice. Shift change was at 0900 hours, and after checking and 'cocking' their jets (ensuring they were ready for immediate launching) they would settle down in the Zulu crew quarters upstairs in the barn. As soon as the klaxon went off, they would slide down firemen's poles, rush to their jets and launch to intercept. If scrambled, it would either be for a 'Tango' (training) or an 'Alpha' (a live intercept, although the latter was usually a lost civilian pilot). On average, pilots could expect to find it their turn to sit Zulu Alert twice a month.

The 26th TRW was at Zweibrücken AB (tailcode 'ZR'). Its single squadron, the 38th TRS (with green/white checkerboard fin stripe), had operated RF-4Cs since 1965 and held twenty-one as of 1989 (the wing's other squadron, the 17th TRS, had inactivated in 1978). When the 1st TRS in the UK ceased operations during 1987, the 38th TRS became USAFE's sole RF-4C tactical recon squadron.

Up until the 1980s the bulk of USAFE's strength was provided by F-4 Phantom IIs; the decade would see F-16s almost entirely replace them to become the most prevalent type in USAFE.

An F-15C of the 22nd TFS, 36th TFW, over Denmark during Danish air defence exercise Oksboel '86. (NARA)

Another view of the 22nd TFS F-15C seen in the previous photograph, again during exercise Oksboel '86. (NARA)

An F-15C and an F-15D of the 22nd TFS, 53rd TFW, taxi at RAF Alconbury during exercise Red Star '87. The exercise, hosted by the 527th AS, employed F-5Es and F-111s to simulate Soviet formations and tactics, providing realistic training for the F-15 Eagle pilots. (NARA)

A pair of RF-4Cs of the 38th TRS, 26th TRW, fly past Burg Hohenzollern during 1985. The aircraft wear the later wraparound version of 'SEA' camouflage (i.e. with the light grey undersides repainted in the upper side camouflage colours) with toned down markings. (NARA)

This 1987 dated image shows a 38th TRS, 26th TRW, RF-4C in wing commander's markings, wearing the 'European I' camouflage scheme that replaced the previous 'SEA' scheme. (NARA)

An RF-4C of the 38th TRS, 26th TRW, lifts off from Aviano Air Base during exercise Display Determination '89, wearing the final 'Hill Gray' camouflage scheme introduced to Phantoms late in the decade. This scheme was a simplified version of the original camouflage scheme used by the F-16. (NARA)

The 50th TFW at Hahn AB ('HR' tailcode) was first to transition from F-4 to F-16. Components were the 10th TFS (blue fin stripe), 313th TFS (white fin stripe, changing to orange during 1986) and the 496th TFS (red fin stripe, changing to yellow during 1986). The 496th TFS had been equipped with F-4Es since 1970, whilst the 10th and 313th received F-4Es in 1976. These were replaced by F-16A/B Block 15s, arriving with the 313th TFS on 30 December 1981. The squadron had previously received some F-16A Block 10s from Hill AFB during late 1980, purely for ground crew familiarisation. By mid-1982, the last F-4Es had left the wing. F-16C/D Block 25s replaced the earlier A/B models with the 10th and 496th TFS from 1986, the 313th TFS following suit in 1988. The wing was due to receive night-attack-capable Block 40 F-16C/Ds (equipped with the new LANTIRN navigation and targeting system) from 1990, but only a single F-16D Block 40 was received before the end of the Cold War shelved those plans. In 1989 the wing operated seventy F-16C Block 25s and six F-16D Block 25s. The wing had a primary air defence role (with AIM-9L/M). It also had a secondary ground attack role (typical F-16 ordnance of the period including Mk 82/84 slick or retarded bombs, cluster bombs and AGM-65 Maverick AGMs). Finally, it had a strike role (with B-43 or B-61 tactical nuclear weapons). USAFE F-16s typically carried AN/ALQ-131 (deep) ECM pods. The 50th TFW maintained a Victor Alert of nuclear armed jets.

A pair of 313th TFS, 50th TFW, F-16A Block 15s carrying deep ALQ-131 ECM pods and SUU-20 practice bomb dispensers during 1982. (NARA)

An F-16A Block 15 of the 10th TFS, 50th TFW, flies over the Pyrenees during 1985. (NARA)

The 496th TFS, 50th TFW, shows off one if its newly received F-16C Block 25s during 1986. An ALQ-131 is on its underside. (NARA)

50th TFW F-16C Block 25s are seen deploying to Zaragoza, Spain, from their home base at Hahn, West Germany, for exercise Sabre Thunder, a weapons training deployment during June 1987. They are supported by a 384th Air Refueling Wing KC-135R doing TDY duty with the ETTF. The foreground F-16C is the wing commander's specially marked bird, whilst 10th TFS jets are seen beyond. As an aside, the following month, the 384th AREFW became the 384th Bombardment Wing when a B-1B squadron was added to the wing. (NARA)

A 50th Aircraft Generation Squadron crew chief looks on as two 10th TFS, 50th TFW, F-16C Block 25s prepare to launch during exercise Sabre Thunder at Zaragoza Air Base. The hangar behind displays the markings of the resident 406th TFTW, which had no aircraft assigned; it instead supported USAFE squadrons deploying to Zaragoza to train at the Bardenas Reales Air-to-Ground Range. (NARA)

Weapons specialists of the 50th Aircraft Generation Squadron load BDU-33 25 lb practice 'blue bombs' into the SUU-20 practice bomb dispenser beneath the wing of a 10th TFS F-16C Block 25 during exercise Sabre Thunder at Zaragoza. (NARA)

The 86th TFW at Ramstein AB, West Germany ('RS' tailcode), had two squadrons: the 512th TFS 'Dragons' (yellow/black checkerboard fin stripe, later switching to green/black stripes) and the 526th TFS 'Black Knights' (red/black checkerboard, later, red/black stripes). From late 1985 the wing started conversion from F-4Es to Pratt & Whitney F100-PW-200-powered F-16C/D Block 25s, but delivery was slow. The decision was taken to switch to further improved General Electric F110-GE-100-powered F-16C/D Block 30s and these were received from late 1986. By 1989 the wing operated forty-eight F-16C Block 30s and two D Block 30s. Small numbers of F-16C/D Block 40s were received in 1990, before the decision was made to inactivate the wing after the end of the Cold War. The wing had a primary air-to-ground role, along with nuclear strike, whilst retaining air-to-air capability and indeed maintained – as mentioned above – a Zulu Alert of aircraft ready to launch on air defence intercepts. During the wing's switch from F-4E to F-16C, the Zulu Alert was covered by specially deployed Air National Guard aircraft under 'Creek Klaxon' (discussed below). The 86th TFW also maintained a 'Victor Alert' of nuclear armed jets. The 86th TFW was also responsible for the Kaiserslautern military community of 50,000 USAF/Army personnel and dependents, a considerable administrative burden. The 377th Combat Support Wing activated at Ramstein in 1985 to take over these responsibilities.

An F-4E of the 526th TFS, 86th TFW, during 1982. It is carrying four AIM-7F Sparrows and four AIM-9P Sidewinders. It wears the 'SEA' camouflage with light grey undersides. (NARA)

A 1983 view of another 526th TFS, 86th TFW, F-4E, this one without squadron-colour fin stripe. It is again carrying AIM-7Fs and AIM-9Ps. Note that it is wearing the late 'wraparound' version of 'SEA' camouflage with the light grey undersides repainted in the upper side colours. This was done as the light grey undersides would reveal the F-4 to hostile aircraft looking down from higher altitudes when it banked into a corner and briefly exposed its light grey undersides, which stood out against the European terrain, to view from above. (NARA)

A pair of F-4Es of the 526th TFS (near) and 512th TFS (far) during 1985, in the twilight of their service with the 86th TFW. Both aircraft carry AIM-7F and AIM-9P missiles. Note that, whilst both aircraft wear wraparound 'SEA' camouflage, the 526th TFS F-4E nearest the camera has received a replacement rudder from another aircraft that was painted in the later 'European I' camouflage scheme in which the former tan colour was replaced by grey. The 512th TFS jet is seen venting fuel. Both jets have appropriate serial numbers for their respective squadrons. (NARA)

Out with the old and in with the new. A 526th TFS, 86th TFW, F-4E in formation with one of its replacement F-16C Block 25s during 1986. The F100-PW-200-powered F-16C/D Block 25s themselves were short lived with the 86th TFW, with the decision soon taken to switch to further improved General Electric F110-GE-100-powered F-16C/D Block 30s. (NARA)

Whilst the 86th TFW transitioned from the F-4E to the F-16C/D, the wing's Zulu Alert air defence responsibilities were covered by a detachment of ANG F-4Ds from 1 March 1986 to 6 April 1987 under Operation Creek Klaxon. Three squadrons (from the California ANG, Minnesota ANG and North Dakota ANG) contributed aircraft whilst all ANG F-4C/D units provided crews on rotation. Here a 526th TFS F-4E in the then new 'European I' camouflage scheme is seen alongside an F-4D of the 'Happy Hooligans', 178th FIS, 119th FIG, North Dakota Air National Guard, in April 1986. Both aircraft are armed with live AIM-7Fs and AIM-9Ps. (NARA)

An F-4D of the 179th FIS, 148th FIG, Minnesota Air National Guard, in the Zulu Alert hangar at Ramstein Air Base during Operation Creek Klaxon in 1987. 'Cocked' and ready to scramble, the jet is armed with live AIM-7F and AIM-9P missiles plus an under fuselage SUU-23 20 mm gun pod. (NARA)

Seen in formation during January 1987 are F-4Ds of the 178th FIS, 119th FIG, North Dakota ANG (nearest), and 179th FIS, 148th FIG, Minnesota ANG, along with a newly received F-16C Block 25 of the 526th TFS that will soon relieve the former of their 'Creek Klaxon' Zulu Alert responsibilities. The F-4Ds carry live AIM-7Fs, AIM-9Ps and an SUU-23 20 mm gun pod whilst the F-16C carries CATM-9P training Sidewinders and a deep ALQ-131 ECM pod. The third ANG F-4D unit to provide aircraft for 'Creek Klaxon' was the 194th FIS, 144th FIW, California ANG. (NARA)

The final F-4/F-16 wing within 17 AF operated in the 'Wild Weasel' SEAD role. The 52nd TFW at Spangdahlem AB ('SP' tail code) was assigned the 23rd TFS 'Fighting Hawks' (blue fin stripe), 81st TFS (yellow fin stripe) and the 480th TFS (red fin stripe). The 23rd TFS replaced its F-4Ds with F-4Es from April 1980, the last F-4Ds leaving in April 1982. The 81st TFS had used 'Wild Weasel IV' F-4Cs until July 1979, the last leaving after being replaced by the definitive and far superior F-4G 'Wild Weasel V'. The 480th TFS replaced its F-4Ds with F-4Es by March 1980. The F-4G was the last front line USAF Phantom II variant introduced, produced by conversion of F-4E airframes. The heart of the new model was the AN/APR-38 RHAW (Radar Homing and Warning) system, part of which displaced the gun from the nose of the former model. This was squadron-reprogrammable, being updateable to recognise all known air defence radar systems, displaying their locations in predetermined priority order to the crew. Targets could then be engaged by anti-radiation missiles (ARMs), initially AGM-45A/B Shrike or AGM-78D Standard missiles, the latter replaced by AGM-88A HARM (High-speed Anti-Radiation Missiles) by 1984. The less effective Shrikes remained in the inventory into the 1990s alongside HARM, and improved AGM-88B HARMs were added by the end of the decade. The limitations of Shrike included that it required different sub-variants of the missile to target different radar systems and the limited range of the missile required it to be fired well within the range of the enemy surface-to-air missile (SAM) sites. HARM addressed these deficiencies, also adding much increased speed, allowing targets to be struck before they could react. F-4Gs could also use the usual range of air-to-ground ordnance, including bombs/cluster bombs, AGM-65 and GBU-15. From 1987 the F-4G's AN/APR-38 RHAW was upgraded to the much improved AN/APR-47 standard, with a threefold increase in computer memory (to 250K) and able to analyse threats five times faster.

An 81st TFS, 52nd TFW, F-4G 'Wild Weasel V', in front of a TAB-V ('Theater Air Base-Vulnerability') aircraft shelter at Spangdahlem AB during 1982. Wearing the wraparound SEA camouflage scheme, the aircraft is armed with AGM-45 Shrike anti-radiation missiles intended to home in on hostile radar. (NARA)

One practical advantage was that F-4Gs would need to spend less time during 'pop ups' from low-level flight in order to acquire targets. This and other improvements resulted in the 'Wild Weasel VI' designation. The expensive and scarce F-4Gs were augmented by the wing's standard F-4Es, operating in 'hunter killer teams' (F-4Gs being the hunters, F-4Es the killers). From December 1983 through May 1984 the wing was reorganised, with each squadron now operating a mixture of F-4Es and Gs, rather than just one model. From September 1987 the F-4Es were replaced by F-16C/D Block 30s in the 'killer' role, continuing to operate alongside the F-4G 'hunters'. By 1989 the wing operated a total of thirty-nine F-4Gs, thirty F-16C Block 30s and three F-16D Block 30s, all split equally between the three squadrons.

The 52nd TFW would have been essential, escorting strike packages, suppressing or destroying enemy ground-based air defences (whilst EF-111As provided jamming and F-15s/F-16s provided fighter escort). The F-4Gs (and EF-111As) offered unique capabilities within NATO forces, and were in short supply.

GLCMs equipped two 17 AF wings, with a third due to form. The 38th TMW at Wüschheim Air Station and component 89th TMS activated on 1 April 1985, receiving sixty-four of the intended ninety-six GLCMs before deliveries were frozen on 9 December 1987, as with all units still equipping, the day after Mikhail Gorbachev and Ronald Reagan signed the INF Treaty. Both wing and squadron inactivated on 22 August 1990.

The 485th TMW at Florennes AB, Belgium, and component 71st TMS activated on 1 August 1984, receiving only sixteen of its allocated forty-eight GLCMs before deliveries stopped. The squadron inactivated on 30 April 1989, the wing on 30 September 1989.

Finally, the 486th TMW activated on 27 August 1987 at Woensdrecht AB, the Netherlands; however, no squadron was assigned and none of the allocated forty-eight missiles were received before the wing inactivated on 30 September 1988.

Seen during 1984, an F-4G leads a pair of F-4Es, all three from the 480th TFS, 52nd TFW. The F-4G carries three AIM-7F Sparrows and a shallow ALQ-131 ECM pod in the forward port Sparrow missile-well as well as an AGM-45 Shrike and an AGM-78 Standard. The far F-4E carries three Sparrows and a deep ALQ-131 under the fuselage, as well as a pair of AGM-45s, whilst the near F-4E carries three Sparrows and a shallow ALQ-131, plus four AIM-9P-3 Sidewinders and six inert Mk 82 500 lb practice bombs (two of which are obscured here). It carries a pair of 370 US gal. underwing fuel tanks, whilst the other two jets both have a centreline 600 US gal. tank. All three wear the 'European I' camouflage scheme, which started to be applied to 52nd TFW Phantoms from mid-1983. (NARA)

Belgian Air Force personnel load live Mk 82 Snakeye bombs on a 480th TFS, 52nd TFW, F-4G during an 'Ample Gain' exercise in 1985 at Bierset AB, Belgium. 'Ample Gain' exercises gave NATO ground crews the opportunity to practice servicing aircraft used by other NATO air forces, an important skill that may have become necessary in wartime. Whilst the foreground F-4G wears 'European I' camouflage, the F-4E behind still wears wraparound 'SEA' camouflage. (NARA)

An F-4G leads a newly received F-16C Block 30 during 1987, both aircraft in 52nd TFW wing commander's markings. The F-4G carries AGM-88 HARM training missiles, a deep ALQ-131 and two AIM-7Fs in the rear wells only as well as both centreline 600 US gal and 370 US gal underwing fuel tanks, whilst the F-16C has CATM-9L captive training Sidewinders and AGM-45 Shrikes as well as (out of view here) a centreline deep ALQ-131 ECM pod. By this time, 52nd TFW F-4Gs were wearing 'Hill Gray' camouflage. This two-tone medium and dark grey scheme was very similar, but not identical, to the three-tone light, medium and dark grey factory-applied scheme worn by F-16s. Much later on, F-16s would adopt the simplified two tone 'Hill Gray' scheme (dropping the light grey undersides in favour of medium grey). (NARA)

Two F-4Gs of the 81st TFS, 52nd TFW, in flight over the English coast during 1988. The furthest aircraft is carrying training versions of the AGM-88A HARM. (NARA)

The same pair of F-4Gs, on the same sortie, as seen in the previous image are now joined by an F-16C Block 30, also of the 81st TFS, 52d TFW, off the coast of Margate, England. The F-16C carries an Acceleration Monitor Assembly (AMA) pod on its port wingtip station, and a CATM-9L training Sidewinder to starboard. (NARA)

The 52nd TFW wing commander's F-16C Block 30 leads the 480th TFS squadron commander's F-4G over West Germany during 1989. Both aircraft carry training versions of the AGM-88 HARM, whilst the F-16C also carries a pair of CATM-9L training Sidewinders and the F-4G carries a pair of AIM-7Fs in the rear wells and a deep ALQ-131 pod in the port forward Sparrow missile well. (NARA)

A GLCM TEL of the Florennes-based 485th Tactical Missile Wing during an exercise in the Belgian countryside. The launcher is raised as crews conduct a simulated launch. The tractor unit of the TEL is a MAN M1014. (NARA)

The 66th ECW at Sembach AB was activated on 1 June 1985, with two flying squadrons assigned. The 42nd ECS at RAF Upper Heyford in 3 AF had been assigned, since activation in 1983, to the resident 20th TFW as outlined above. However, the 42nd ECS was reassigned to the 66th ECW upon the latter's activation, but this was purely administrative and the 42nd ECS remained at Upper Heyford, attached to, and under the operational control of, the 20th TFW. The other squadron, the 43rd ECS, activated on 1 October 1986. It was equipped with the EC-130H 'Compass Call' (seven on strength as of 1989) using the 'SB' tailcode. The EC-130H 'Compass Call' was a communications jamming aircraft, disrupting enemy command and control communications, limiting their ability to manage their forces, especially air forces.

Also at Sembach, the 601st Tactical Control Wing (TCW) was not primarily a flying unit, being responsible for controlling air operations, through operating AN/TPS-43 mobile radars and ground-based FACs. USAFE's largest wing, half of its 6,000 personnel were spread from northern Italy to the North Sea, many attached to US Army units, calling in CAS from their jeeps during exercises – as they would in wartime. However, it also controlled the 601st Tactical Air Support Group (TASG), which in turn controlled the 20th and 704th Tactical Air Support Squadrons (TASS) – operating forty-five FAC OV-10A Broncos – and the 601st TASS – with six CH-53Cs, used to air deliver the AN/TPS-43 mobile radars. The OV-10A, becoming too vulnerable over the Central Front battlefield, was relegated to a wartime role of loitering over the rear of the battlefield (normally only with a pilot and no back seater) relaying radio messages from ground FACs to A-10As and other CAS aircraft. The OV-10A units inactivated on 30 September 1984, after squadron aircrews had ferried their aircraft to George AFB, California, during June–August 1984. The CH-53C-equipped 601st TASS inactivated during 1988, leaving the 601st TCW without aircraft.

As noted in the 3 AF section, UK-based A-10As were permanently forward-deployed to four FOLs in West Germany under 17 AF, increasing to six FOLs under NATO in wartime.

Five Munitions Support Squadrons, holding tactical nuclear weapons for wartime allied use, were under 17 AF: the 7261st MSS, Memmingen AB, West Germany, for use by JBG 34 of the Luftwaffe (with F-104G, later Tornado); the 7361st MSS,

Flight engineer Technical Sergeant Kenneth Hiller and flight evaluator Captain Griffin Drees, both from the 43rd ECS, and pilot Major John Ferrell, of the 66th ECW, watch the horizon from the cockpit of their EC-130H 'Compass Call' communications jamming aircraft for a KC-135A Stratotanker that is to refuel them during 1987. (NARA)

The EC-130H 'Compass Call' from the previous image eases towards a 509th Bombardment Wing KC-135A deployed from Pease AFB, New Hampshire, on TDY with the ETTF. (NARA)

This 1987 view of a 43rd ECS, 66th ECW, EC-130H 'Compass Call' over West Germany shows off the variant's recognition features of ram air inlets both extending forward of, and above, the normal C-130 undercarriage fairing, the blisters either side of the rear fuselage and the tail-mounted wire antenna arrays. (NARA)

A 43rd ECS, 66th ECW, EC-130H 'Compass Call' at Sembach AB during exercise Central Enterprise '89. The ram air inlets are again notable, along with the rear fuselage blisters and support struts below the tail for the antenna arrays. Note the prop tip vortices being created in the humid air. (NARA)

Two OV-10A Broncos of the 601st TASG, in 'European I' camouflage, during exercise Reforger '81. (NARA)

Two CH-53Cs of the 601st TASS, 601st TASG, airlifting equipment during exercise Urex '82. Both wear 'SEA' camouflage with high-visibility markings. (NARA)

Another 601st TASS, 601st TASG, CH-53C during exercise Urex '82, this one has been repainted in 'European I' camouflage with toned-down markings. In the background another CH-53C in 'SEA' camouflage approaches with a slung-load. (NARA)

Kleine Brogel AB, Belgium, for use by 10th Tactical Wing of the Belgian Air Force (with F-104G, later F-16A); the 7362nd MSS, Volkel AB, the Netherlands, for use by Nos 311/312 squadrons of the Royal Netherlands Air Force (with F-104G, later F-16A); the 7501st MSS, Büchel, West Germany, for use by JBG 33 of the Luftwaffe (F-104G, later Tornado IDS); and finally, the 7502nd MSS, Nörvenich, West Germany, for wartime use by JBG 31 of the Luftwaffe (F-104G, later Tornado IDS).

The 7005th Air Base Squadron operated Stuttgart Army Airfield and had two C-12C and three C-21A light transport aircraft by 1989.

In June 1985, two Air Divisions were activated in 17 AF. The 65th Air Division at Lindsey Air Station, with responsibility for integrating USAFE's electronic combat systems, took control of the 52nd TFW, 66th ECW and 601st TCW. The 316th Air Division at Ramstein took control of the co-located 86th TFW and administrative 377th CSW.

Direct Reporting

The most notable, and shadowy, unit that reported directly to USAFE headquarters was the 7575th Operations Group (OG) at Rhein-Main AB. It controlled the 7th Special Operations Squadron (SOS) with four MC-130E-C (Clamp) Combat Talon Is, which would have dropped and resupplied special forces behind enemy lines in wartime. In 1983 the unit was reassigned from USAFE to Military Airlift Command (MAC), whilst remaining in place (q.v.). Even more covert was the 7405th Operations

An MC-130E-C Combat Talon I of the 7th SOS, 7575th OG, during a Fulton recovery training mission over West Germany in 1980. Note the special green and black camouflage scheme used by MC-130Es at this time. (NARA)

Later in the mission from the previous image, a controller coordinates with the MC-130E-C Combat Talon I by radio as the aircraft approaches a Fulton recovery balloon. On a subsequent pass the aircraft will snare the line held aloft by the balloon with its Fulton STARS (Surface-To-Air Recovery System) lifting the training load, which will subsequently be winched aboard. (NARA)

Squadron, operating three C-130E Hercules. These were not standard transports, but were modified with cameras, infra-red and signals intelligence (SIGINT) sensors and operated along the East German air corridors to Tempelhof in West Berlin. They wore fake MAC markings and appeared no different to standard transports plying the same routes. In hindsight, the Soviets and East Germans were well aware of their activities, but they are reputed to have gleaned much useful intelligence. Finally, the 7575th OG controlled the 7580th Operations Squadron, a non-flying squadron staffed with C-130 Electronic Warfare Officers (EWOs) and aircraft maintenance personnel.

The 7350th Air Base Group was responsible for operations at Tempelhof Airport, West Berlin. The remainder of USAFE's direct reporting units were non-flying.

Supporters from Stateside

Other USAF commands committed aircraft to Europe, supporting USAFE, generally sending them on rotational Temporary Duty (TDY) deployments from US-based units.

Strategic Air Command (SAC)

European-based SAC assets were reorganised during 1978. The 7th Air Division was activated at Ramstein on 1 July, controlling SAC units in Europe and acting as the advanced echelon for wartime reinforcements, and the 306th Strategic Wing moved to RAF Mildenhall overseeing TDY tanker and RC-135 strategic reconnaissance aircraft deployments. Typically, there would be around sixteen TDY tankers (including ANG and AFRES KC-135s) at Mildenhall. There would also usually be two or three RC-135U/V/W strategic reconnaissance aircraft in Europe at any one time at Mildenhall, Hellenikon and elsewhere. Also under the 306th SW was the 34th Strategic Squadron (SS) with the KC-135, later KC-10, at Zaragoza AB, Spain, and the 922nd SS at Hellenikon Air Base, Greece (with KC-/RC-135s).

Also activated in 1978 was the 11th Strategic Group at RAF Fairford, usually supporting around fifteen TDY tankers. The 34th SS at Zaragoza AB transferred from 306th SW to 11th SG control on 1 October 1986. Further 11th SG detachments were made to Riyadh (Saudi Arabia), Keflavik (Iceland), Lajes Field (Azores) and NAS Sigonella (Sicily). Each of these forward detachments normally involved a couple of aircraft. In the early 1980s the 11th SG Det at Keflavik became Det 1 of the 306th SW.

The 306th SW and 11th SG tanker assets made up the European Tanker Task Force (ETTF). KC-135As were most common, although throughout the 1980s ANG/AFRES KC-135Es and SAC KC-135Rs were increasingly seen. KC-135Qs would also be assigned, supporting SR-71 operations, whilst occasionally KC-10As were deployed, notably for Operation El Dorado Canyon in 1986 and periodic B-52 deployments to Fairford. The Zaragoza det replaced its KC-135s with KC-10s from 1985. Operations staff, maintenance personnel and some instructor pilots were permanently assigned, but aircraft, aircrews and crew chiefs were assigned on a TDY basis to the ETTF. TDYs typically lasted around forty-five days, sometimes shorter. UK-based KC-135s also often supported RAF QRA air defence aircraft (requiring fitment of a drogue adaptor to their flying boom to do so) and NATO E-3 Sentry AWACS aircraft.

The 9th Strategic Reconnaissance Wing (SRW) at Beale AFB, CA, maintained detachments in Europe. The 100th SRW took over the CIA's U-2R 'Det G' at RAF Akrotiri, Cyprus, in 1974 as Operating Location Olive Harvest (OL-OH). U-2 operations moved from the 100th SRW to the 9th SRW in 1976, OL-OH falling

A SAC KC-135A on TDY with the European Tanker Task Force (ETTF) refuels a pair of 313th TFS, 50th TFW, F-16As during 1982. (NARA)

A KC-135E of the Utah Air National Guard (191st Air Refueling Squadron, 151st Air Refueling Group) on TDY with the ETTF, over the English Channel during 1987. The Pratt & Whitney TF-33-PW-102 engines with which the KC-135E model was re-engined can clearly be seen here, when compared to the 'stovepipe' Pratt & Whitney J57s on the KC-135A in the previous image. (NARA)

An RC-135W 'Rivet Joint' on TDY with the 306th Strategic Wing at RAF Mildenhall during 1988, being refuelled over the North Sea by a KC-135R of the 912th AREFS, 19th AREFW, also on TDY with the 306th SW/ETTF. (NARA)

An RC-135V 'Rivet Joint' on TDY with the 306th Strategic Wing during 1989. (NARA)

under the latter from then on, carrying out missions over the Middle East, including monitoring the stand-off between Egypt and Israel on behalf of the United Nations. The 1978 Camp David peace accords formalised this monitoring, with the reconnaissance 'take' shared between all parties involved. OL-OH became Det 3, 9th SRW, in September 1980, usually operating two U-2Rs.

Detachment 4 of the 9th SRW was established in April 1979 at RAF Mildenhall with a single U-2R in the 'Creek Spectre' SIGINT role; previously, only TDY U-2 deployments had been made. Det 4 also supported periodic SR-71A deployments – the UK Government stipulated that early SR-71 deployments should be no longer than twenty days, each sortie requiring UK permission. In February 1983 Det 4 ceased U-2R operations after the 17th RW became operational with the TR-1A (q.v.). In 1984 Prime Minister Thatcher agreed that Det 4 would become a permanent SR-71A detachment with two aircraft.

On 18 June 1987 a Det 4 SR-71 on a routine mission in the Barents/Baltic seas suffered an explosion in the right engine during its run along the Soviet coast. Whilst speed and altitude were the SR-71's only defence, the crew – Majors Duane Noll (pilot) and Tom Veltri (Reconnaissance Systems Officer) – found themselves going from 80,000 feet at Mach 3 to 25,000 feet and 437 mph in a matter of minutes. As they headed for safety and declared an emergency, the Soviets launched around twenty interceptors with orders to force the SR-71 to land in Soviet territory or shoot them down. Fortunately, neutral Swedish Air Force Viggens intercepted the stricken spy plane before the Soviets could intercept; a few minutes later a Soviet MiG-25 arrived on the scene, shadowing the US/Swedish formation from a few miles out before departing. The Swedish jets escorted the SR-71 along the Polish and East German coasts to just short of NATO (Danish) airspace, where 36th TFW F-15s took over

An SR-71A assigned to Det. 4, 9th Strategic Reconnaissance Wing, prepares to take off from RAF Mildenhall during 1988. (NARA)

the escort, the SR-71 diverting to Nordholz in West Germany. The wind-down of the Cold War saw the last Det 4 SR-71 mission flown on 20 September 1989, with Det 4 closing down in early 1990.

In order not to be overwhelmed by superior enemy numbers in wartime, NATO needed to concentrate its firepower where the enemy was massing its forces for the attack. Effective reconnaissance deep into the WarPac rear, under the control of theatre commanders, was essential. The intelligence generated needed to be made immediately available to commanders so that forces could be correctly deployed and air strikes made against the enemy concentrations. US spy satellites could not see through cloud and were controlled through the highly classified Washington-based National Reconnaissance Office. SR-71s had cameras plus, from 1983, the ASARS-1 radar (an all-weather, day/night, real-time, high-resolution reconnaissance system capable of mapping and accurately locating stationary and moving ground targets). However, SR-71s were scarce, costly and not controlled by local commanders. Therefore in 1978 the decision was taken to put the U-2R back into production (the original 1960s-produced batch of twelve aircraft was by then down to just nine airframes), not only to bolster existing U-2R numbers, but also to take on the European high-altitude tactical reconnaissance mission. Those intended for the latter mission unusually received a new designation – TR-1A – despite being identical to the U-2R, in a bid to distance the type from the 'spyplane' stereotype. From 1981 twenty-four TR-1As and three TR-1B trainers were built (plus a pair of ER-2 NASA research aircraft and, from separate 'black' funds, seven U-2Rs and a U-2RT trainer to augment the original fleet).

The 17th Reconnaissance Wing, and component 95th Reconnaissance Squadron, activated on 1 October 1982 at RAF Alconbury and received the first TR-1A on 12 February 1983, slowly building up its fleet. Although a SAC unit, it fell under peacetime USAFE control and in wartime would have been under NATO control.

Along with tactical recon, the unit's TR-1As took on the Creek Spectre strategic SIGINT mission, allowing Det 4, 9th SRW, to cease U-2R operations in February 1983. As well as existing strategic recon systems, new sensor systems were developed. There was a failed project to use TR-1As to find SEAD targets, involving the aborted Precision Location Strike System (PLSS). The key system (introduced from 1985) for TR-1A tactical recon would be ASARS-2, similar to the SR-71's ASARS-1, the system's antenna located in a distinctively shaped long nose. This finally provided tactical commanders with timely intelligence round the clock, irrespective of weather or light. The TR-1A's sensors were linked in real time via datalink to the trailer-based TREDS (TR-1 Exploitation Demonstration System – codenamed 'Metro Tango') ground station at Hahn AB. The end of the Cold War came before the definitive – underground and hardened – TRIGS (TR-1 Ground Stations) were fielded, resulting in their cancellation (in favour of the deployable Contingency Airborne Reconnaissance System/Deployable Ground Station – CARS/DGS). By 1989 the 95th RS had nine TR-1As and a single TR-1B on strength.

SAC controlled the non-flying 19th Surveillance Squadron at Pirinclik Air Station, Turkey. It used the AN/FPS-17 Space Surveillance Radar to detect objects in space with fixed antennae oriented towards the Soviet rocket launch and development site at Kapustin Yar and the FPS-79 UHF tracking radar, capable of tracking Soviet missile tests. The squadron was reassigned to 1st Space Wing on 1 May 1983 under newly formed Space Command (later Air Force Space Command).

In wartime, SAC would have utilised a number of Forward Operating Bases (FOBs) for B-52s and FB-111As, including Brize Norton, Fairford, Marham and Upper Heyford, plus Morón in Spain (which would have also probably received KC-135s as well as B-52s).

The first production TR-1A is rolled out at the Palmdale 'Skunk Works' on 15 July 1981. SAC's newly formed 95th RS, 17th RW, received its first TR-1A at RAF Alconbury on 12 February 1983. (NARA)

A TR-1A on a test flight near San
Francisco during 1985. (NARA)

Military Airlift Command (MAC)

MAC's airlifter fleet was split between Twenty-First Air Force (21 AF, HQ McGuire AFB, NJ) controlling resources east of the Mississippi and Twenty-Second Air Force (22 AF: HQ Travis AFB, CA) controlling those to the west. Consequently, 21 AF controlled MAC units forward deployed to Europe.

The 322nd Airlift Division at Ramstein controlled 21 AF's European assets (and, from 1985, responsibility for airlift management in Africa). Reporting directly to 322nd AD at the outset of the 1980s was the 58th Military Airlift Squadron (MAS) at Ramstein with a mixed fleet of C-12A, C-135B, VC-140B and CT-39A aircraft in 1980. Also under direct control was the 608th Military Airlift Support Squadron (MASS), also at Ramstein. This has no aircraft and operated the MAC aerial port, servicing, loading and unloading transient C-5s and C-141s and receiving airlifted equipment and personnel for United States Army Europe units in Germany. On 1 July 1983 the 608th MASS was expanded into the 608th Military Airlift Group (MAG) and took control of the 58th MAS on 1 August 1983. By 1989 58th MAS operated six C-12Fs, three C-20As, three C-21As, a T-43A, a C-135B and six UH-1Ns.

Also assigned to the 608th MAG was the 10th MAS, activated on 15 January 1984. Based at Zweibrücken AB, the 10th MAS used the C-23A for the 'European Distribution System' (EDS), primarily concerned with ferrying aircraft parts, including fighter engines, between USAFE bases in order to help keep the fighter fleet flying.

Eighteen C-23As were delivered to 10th MAS between 2 November 1984 and 7 December 1985. Zweibrücken housed a large aircraft spares warehouse, with a second at RAF Kemble in the UK and a third at Torrejón. This network reduced the need to fly in spares from the USA and any spare part at a European warehouse could be delivered to any location in Europe within 36 hours, in peacetime or wartime. EDS cargoes too large for C-23s were flown in MAC C-130s. The highly efficient C-23As also supported the USN in Europe (transporting items too large for USN C-12s, but not large enough to warrant a USN C-130) and had a wartime contingency role of handling US Army cargo.

The busiest US European air terminal was Rhein-Main AB, West Germany, home to the 435th Tactical Airlift Wing (TAW). Components were the 37th TAS – with around eighteen C-130E transports – and the 55th Aeromedical Airlift Squadron (AAS) – with C-9A Nightingales. The 55th had six C-9As, four in standard aeromedical evacuation configuration and two in VIP transport configuration. A seventh (VIP-configured) C-9A was used by Det 1, HQ, 435th TAW, detached at Chièvres AB, Belgium, for use by NATO's Supreme Allied Commander.

MAC C-141B Starlifters drop 82nd Airborne Division paratroopers over West Germany during exercise Reforger '80. In the right foreground, air traffic controllers from the 82nd coordinate with the aircraft above. (NARA)

A C-141B Starlifter of the 60th MAW from Travis AFB, California, has just delivered men of the 2nd and 4th Battalions, 63rd Armor, 1st Infantry, to Rhein-Main AB, West Germany, for exercise Reforger '82. (NARA)

A 58th MAS C-12A at
Ramstein during 1980.
(NARA)

A 10th MAS,
608th MAG, C-23A seen
during 1985. Each C-23A
was named for a USAFE
base, this one being
Zaragoza. (NARA)

A 37th TAS, 435th
TAW, C-130E in 'SEA'
camouflage during a 1981
flight out of Rhein-Main.
(NARA)

C-130Es of the 37th TAS
at Rhein-Main about to
board paratroopers of the
82nd Airborne Division,
deployed from Fort Bragg,
North Carolina, for exercise
Carbine Fortress in 1982.
The 37th TAS maintained
a proportion of its C-130E
fleet in 'Asia Minor' desert
camouflage during the
1980s for Middle Eastern
or Iranian operational
contingencies. (NARA)

Another 37th TAS C-130E
in 'Asia Minor' desert
camouflage at Rhein-Main
in 1983. (NARA)

C-130Es of the 37th TAS
in more locally appropriate
'European I' camouflage.
The aircraft with engines
running is preparing
for deployment from
Rhein-Main during an
Operational Readiness
Inspection of the
435th TAW in 1984.
(NARA)

A 'European I' clad 37th TAS C-130E landing on the grass strip at Drop Zone Juliet near Aviano AB, Italy, during an evening training mission in 1989. (NARA)

The other major European transport hub was RAF Mildenhall. There, the 313th Tactical Airlift Group (TAG) supported US-based C-130 squadrons (from the 314th, 317th and 463rd TAWs) deployed to Europe. Normally, around sixteen Hercules were deployed. The 313th TAG also controlled the 627th Military Airlift Support Squadron (MASS) until it inactivated on 1 August 1983. Without aircraft, it provided en route support to C-5 and C-141 flights transiting Mildenhall. After the 627th inactivated, other Group elements assumed its mission.

Two other units supported airlift operations under direct 21 AF control: 625th MASS at Torrejón and 628th MASS at Incirlik. On 1 August 1983 the 625th MASS deactivated, replaced by the 625th Military Airlift Support Group.

As well as 21 and 22 AF, MAC also controlled the Aerospace Rescue and Recovery Service, under which was the 39th Aerospace Rescue and Recovery Wing (ARRW) at Eglin AFB, Florida, with a Combat Search and Rescue (CSAR) role. That wing's 67th Aerospace Rescue and Recovery Squadron (ARRS) at RAF Woodbridge had (in 1980) eight HH-53C rescue helicopters plus rescue Hercules: five HC-130N/P models (four and one respectively) which could also refuel the HH-53Cs in-flight and a single HC-130H which could not. The 67th also maintained Det 2 at Ramstein with four UH-1Ns, Det 9 at Zaragoza with three UH-1Ns and Det 14 with HH-3Es at Keflavik. Rotational deployments of HC-130N/Ps supported Det 14 at Keflavik.

Considerable reorganisation followed. On 1 March 1983 MAC activated Twenty-Third Air Force (23 AF), absorbing the responsibilities of the Aerospace Rescue and Recovery Service, with a primary focus on Special Operations support, including (from 1 October 1983) the 39th ARRW/67th ARRS. On 1 March 1983 the MC-130E Combat Talon I-equipped 7th SOS at Rhein-Main AB, heretofore under the 7575th OG/USAFE HQ (see above), was reassigned to 2nd Air Division of 23AF, becoming a MAC asset, then on 1 February 1987 it was further reassigned to 39th ARRW.

On 1 March 1988 39th ARRW became 39th Special Operations Wing (SOW), and the 67th ARRS was split. The rotary wing (H-53) assets moved to the new 21st Special Operations Squadron (SOS), which activated on 1 May 1988, and the fixed wing (HC-130) assets stayed with the 67th, which became the 67th SOS on 1 June 1988. During 1988 the UH-1N-equipped Det 2 at Ramstein and Det 9 at Zaragoza deactivated.

Det 14, 67th ARRS – with the HH-3E at Keflavik – became the 56th ARRS on 1 May 1988, still under 39th SOW. On 1 April 1989 it was reassigned to the 41st Rescue and Weather Reconnaissance Wing (headquartered at McClellan Air Force Base, CA) and redesignated 56th Air Rescue Squadron on 1 June 1989. (The 41st Rescue and Weather Reconnaissance Wing itself was redesignated the Air Rescue Service in August 1989).

39th SOW wing HQ moved from Eglin to Rhein-Main AB on 1 June 1989. By late 1989 the 39th SOW had the following flying units: 7th SOS at Rhein-Main (four MC-130E Combat Talon I); 21st SOS at RAF Woodbridge (with four MH-53J 'Pave Low III Enhanced', plus a HH-53B and three CH-53Cs, plus a further three CH-53Cs located at Sembach); 67th SOS at RAF Woodbridge (with an HC-130H, five HC-130Ns and three HC-130Ps).

Of those types, perhaps most notable was the MH-53J. Arriving with the 21st SOS during 1988, this much upgraded HH/MH-53 was equipped with systems allowing it to penetrate behind enemy lines during the worst weather conditions, supporting SOF, or conducting CSAR.

A HC-130H of the 67th ARRS at RAF Woodbridge during 1981 in 'SEA' camouflage. During the 1980s, many HC-130H and HC-130P aircraft had the nose Fulton recovery gear removed, as is the case with this aircraft. (NARA)

A 67th ARRS HH-53C in 'SEA' camouflage at RAF Woodbridge during 1981. (NARA)

A HH-53C Super Jolly Green Giant of the 67th ARRS overflies Tower Bridge, London, during 1982; this particular aircraft was already repainted in 'European I' camouflage. (NARA)

A HC-130P refuels an HH-53C during a 1982 pararescue training sortie. Both of these 67th ARRS aircraft still wear 'SEA' camouflage. This HC-130P has also had its Fulton recovery gear removed. (NARA)

A 67th ARRS HH-53C, in 'European I' camouflage, about to refuel during exercise Flintlock '87, a Joint Special Operations Command Europe exercise. (NARA)

An HH-53C and, in the background, a HC-130N, both of the 67th ARRS, whilst deployed to Zaragoza during exercise Flintlock '87. (NARA)

Left: A pre-flight check is performed on a 7th SOS MC-130E-C Combat Talon I during exercise Flintlock '87, a Joint Special Operations Command Europe exercise. The 7th SOS was transferred from USAFE (7575th OG) control to MAC, initially to MAC's 2nd Air Division on 1 March 1983, then, two months before this April 1987 photograph, further reassigned to MAC's 39th ARRW on 1 February 1987. This view shows off the radically remodelled nose of the variant plus the 'European I' camouflage used by this stage. (NARA)

Below: Another view of the flight line during exercise Flintlock '87, with an MC-130E-C Combat Talon I showing off its open Fulton 'whiskers'. (NARA)

A 7th SOS MC-130E-C
Combat Talon I during a
1988 sortie. (NARA)

On the same sortie as
the previous image, the
MC-130E-C Combat
Talon I refuels from a
SAC KC-10A on TDY
with the Zaragoza-based
34th Strategic Squadron.
(NARA)

On 1 March 1988 the
rotary wing elements
of the 67th ARRS were
split away to form the
21st SOS. Here, 21st SOS
crews push a newly
arrived MH-53J 'Pave
Low III Enhanced' at
RAF Woodbridge. These
MH-53Js were the first
to arrive in Europe and
are seen on 23 October
1988; they offered much
expanded capability
when compared to the
HH-53Cs operated until
then. (NARA)

A newly received MH-53J
of the 21st SOS in-flight
off the English coast in
November 1988. (NARA)

During 1989 the USAF split its SOF and SAR units, until now under 23 AF. In August 1989 SAR units (including 56th ARS above) transferred to the newly established Air Rescue Service, reporting directly to MAC, whilst SOF remained under 23 AF, which was redesignated Air Force Special Operations Command and elevated to major command status on 22 May 1990.

On 1 October 1987 MAC took on flight inspection (calibrating and evaluating navigational aids) from AFCC; consequently Det 2 of the 1467th Facility Checking Squadron (FCS) – a component of the 375th Aeromedical Airlift Wing at Scott AFB, IL – took on the role, and a single T-39A aircraft, of AFCC's former 1868th FCS at Rhein Main AB (q.v.).

Also under MAC was the Air Weather Service, which provided weather and meteorological services to all branches of the US military in Europe through the 2nd Weather Wing (WW) at Kapaun AS, West Germany, with dets at European USAFE and US Army airfields.

Air Force Communications Command (AFCC)

AFCC's only flying unit in Europe was the 1868th Facility Checking Squadron (FCS) at Rhein Main AB with one T-39A. On 1 October 1987 the mission was transferred to MAC and 1868th FCS became Det 2, 1467th FCS (see above).

Tactical Air Command (TAC), Air National Guard (ANG) and Air Force Reserve (AFRES)

TAC, ANG and AFRES aircraft regularly deployed to Europe for competitions, trials and exercising their wartime reinforcement role. USAFE planned in wartime to almost triple its strength to eighty-eight squadrons as part of Operation Reforger.

Due to the budgetary pressures of the Vietnam War, and as part of a wider forces reduction which saw 35,000 US troops withdraw from Europe, USAFE withdrew the

Exercise Coronet Falcon, which took place between 24 February and 19 March 1981, was the first F-16 overseas deployment to Europe. It was conducted by TAC's 4th TFS, 388th TFW, and consisted of eleven F-16As and a single F-16B, all early Block 5 and Block 10 machines, which deployed from Hill AFB, Utah, to Flesland Air Station, Norway. Here some of the aircraft are seen being refuelled on 1 March 1981, whilst in the foreground are CATM-9P training Sidewinders waiting to be loaded. (NARA)

49th TFW (7th/8th/9th TFS) from Spangdahlem, and the 417 TFS (which went on to join the 49th TFW) from Ramstein, moving them to Holloman AFB under TAC in 1968. These F-4D-equipped units were termed 'dual-based', ready to immediately return to Germany in an emergency. The return of these units was regularly practiced under exercise 'Crested Cap'. When the 49th TFW took on the air superiority role with the F-15 in 1977, the F-4E-equipped 4th TFW took over the 'Crested Cap' commitments, whilst other units would also go on to make the month-long 'Crested Caps' to West Germany.

However, far more units would need to deploy to Europe (and not just to Germany) to meet the wartime requirements and combat coded US-based units (TAC, ANG and AFRES) would periodically make deployments to Europe for (usually) two-week periods, familiarising themselves with European bases and conditions as well as the act of deploying. These were known as 'Coronet', part of the 'Checkered Flag' programme (for tactical or recon units) or 'Salty Bee' (exclusively for recon units). Whilst some of these deployments were made to existing USAFE air bases, known as Major Operating Bases (MOBs), many more bases were required to house all deploying units in wartime. These Collocated Operating Bases (COBs) were bases used by NATO allies, at which USAF munitions storage, refuelling and maintenance facilities were added for wartime use by deploying aircraft in a USAF-administered scheme. Aircraft deploying to COBs would usually make use of dispersed parking, not generally having the benefit of hardened shelters. Further 'Standby Operating Bases' were established at little-used or unused air bases.

'Crested Cap', 'Coronet' and 'Salty Bee' deployments made to European bases during the 1980s indicating likely wartime stationing; command/types involved in those deployments are therefore noted in parenthesis in the following description of COBs.

In the UK, COBs were RAF stations at Coltishall (ANG RF-4Cs), Finningley (ANG F-4Ds), Waddington (ANG A-7D/Ks) and Wittering (ANG A-7D/Ks), these having 'Special Storage Areas' for tactical nuclear weapons. Other UK COBs were Bedford, Benson, Boscombe Down (27 TFW F-111Ds/390 ECS EF-111As), Cranwell, Leeming (ANG F-4Cs) and Odiham. USAFE MOBs also received deployments: Alconbury (TAC/ANG RF-4Cs), Bentwaters (TAC F-16A/Bs until 1985, TAC A-10As from 1986)

Coronet Musket saw the deployment of twelve F-4Es of the 335th TFS, 4th TFW (TAC), from Seymour-Johnson AFB, North Carolina, to Karup AB, Denmark, from 12 August to 2 September 1982. Here, four of the deployed F-4Es are seen over Denmark on 14 August 1982. (NARA)

A 335th TFS F-4E crew walks out to their jet at Karup AB, Denmark, during Coronet Musket. (NARA)

A trio of 335th TFS F-4Es during Coronet Musket in Denmark. (NARA)

Seven of the twelve deployed 335th TFS F-4Es are seen on the flight line at Karup AB during Coronet Musket. (NARA)

and Woodbridge (TAC A-10As, plus two deployments by 4450th TG A-7Ds, this unit's main equipment being the then-secret F-117A, indicating possible wartime deployment of that type to Woodbridge). 'Standby Operating Bases' in the UK were Greenham Common, Sculthorpe (ANG A-7Ds) and Wethersfield (ANG A-10As).

In West Germany wartime deployment bases were Ahlhorn (AFRES A-10As), CFB Baden-Söllingen (TAC F-15A/Bs), Bremgarten (TAC F-15s), Erding, Hohn (TAC/ANG A-10As), Ingolstadt-Manching (ANG RF-4Cs), CFB Lahr (TAC F-15s), Lechfeld (ANG A-10As), Leck (TAC A-10As), Nordholz (TAC/ANG A-10As), Rheine-Hopsten (ANG F-4Es), RAF Wildenrath (TAC F-4Gs/ANG F-4Ds) and Wittmundhafen (TAC F-4Es, F-15A/Bs, ANG A-7D/Ks). Also to be used were Jever (TAC F-4E/Gs), Leipheim (ANG A-10As) and Nörvenich (AFRES A-10As) – these three bases also to be used by USAFE A-10s in wartime as noted above. USAFE MOBs also saw deployments: Ramstein (TAC F-4Es, F-16A/Bs, periodic E-3 deployments), Sembach (AFRES A-10As), Spangdahlem (ANG F-4Ds, A-7D/Ks) and Zweibrücken (TAC/ANG RF-4Cs).

Available in Belgium were Brustem (ANG A-7D/Ks) and Koksijde. The USAFE MOB at Chièvres (operated by the 7104th ABG) was also to receive reinforcements. In the Netherlands Gilze-Rijen (TAC F-15A/Bs) was available, as well as the Soesterberg MOB (TAC F-15s).

In Norway COBs were Andøya (ANG F-4Cs, Alaskan Air Command A-10As), Bardufoss (ANG RF-4Cs), Bergen-Flesland (TAC F-16A/Bs), Bodø (AFRES F-4Cs, TAC F-16s, ANG F-4Es), Evenes (ANG A-7Ds), Ørland (ANG A-7Ds, TAC F-16As), Oslo-Gardermoen (TAC F-16As), Rygge (TAC/ANG F-16As), Stavanger-Sola (ANG F-4D/Es) and Trondheim-Værnes (Alaskan Air Command F-4Es). COBs in Denmark were Ålborg (TAC F-15s), Karup (TAC F-4Es, ANG RF-4Cs), Skrydstrup (AFRES F-105D/F, later F-16A/B) and Vandel (AFRES A-10As).

In Spain was Rota (ANG F-4Cs) plus Morón AB maintained as a Standby Deployment Base (SDB) by Det 2, 401 TFW (which became the 7120th Air Base Flight under 16 AF on 1 November 1989). In Italy, Ghedi (TAC F-16A/Bs), Gioia del Colle (ANG A-7D/Ks, TAC F-16A/Bs) and Verona Villafranca (AFRES A-10A) were available, plus the Aviano MOB (TAC/ANG RF-4Cs, ANG F-4Es).

Coronet Wrangler saw the deployment of eleven Block 10 F-16As and one F-16B of the 429th TFS, 474th TFW, from Nellis AFB, Nevada, to RAF Bentwaters, UK, between 13 April and 7 May 1982. This was a troubled deployment, as in mid-April USAF F-16s which had completed more than 200 hours were grounded and the planned involvement by the 429th TFS in RAF air defence exercise 'Elder Forest' was cancelled. Then, on 4 May one of their F-16As crashed near Beccles, Norfolk; fortunately, the pilot ejected safely. Here an F-16A is seen being pushed back into a TAB-V shelter at Bentwaters. (NARA)

Coronet Cactus saw the 110th TFS, 131 TFW, Missouri ANG, deploy twelve F-4C Phantom IIs from St Louis, Missouri, to RAF Leeming, UK, from 26 June to 9 July 1982. (NARA)

RAF personnel undertaking NBC decontamination training on a 110th TFS, Missouri ANG, F-4C at RAF Leeming on 26 June 1982 during Coronet Cactus. (NARA)

Held from 6 to 16 September 1982, Coronet Rawhide involved the 141st TFS, 108th TFG, of the New Jersey ANG deploying twelve F-4Ds from McGuire AFB to Sola Air Station, Norway. Here, Staff Sergeant Roberto Quinones packs a drag chute into the rear of an F-4D. (NARA)

Here, a pair of New Jersey ANG F-4Ds are flying in formation with a Luftforsvaret (Royal Norwegian Air Force) F-5A during Coronet Rawhide. (NARA)

In Greece were Araxos (ANG A-7D/Ks) and Nea Ankhialos (TAC F-4Es). Finally, in Turkey were Akhisar (TAC/ANG F-16s), Balikesir (ANG F-4Cs), Bandirma (TAC A-10As), Eskişehir (ANG F-4Cs, RF-4Cs, A-10As), Izmir-Çigli (AFRES F-4Ds), Merzifon (ANG A-7Ds), Murted (ANG F-105Gs), Sivrihisar (AFRES F-4Ds, ANG A-7Ds) and Yenişehir (TAC/ANG A-10As).

From 1 March 1986 to 6 April 1987 'Creek Klaxon' saw the deployment from the US to Ramstein of nine F-4D Phantoms (not all in-country at once) from three ANG squadrons to stand alert duties whilst the Ramstein-based 86th TFW converted from F-4Es to the F-16C/Ds. All ANG F-4C/D units provided crews on rotation, the F-4Ds coming from 119th Fighter Interceptor Group (FIG)/178th Fighter Interceptor Squadron (FIS), North Dakota ANG; 144th Fighter Interceptor Wing (FIW)/194th FIS, California ANG; and the 148th FIG/179th FIS, Minnesota ANG. The 86th TFW resumed alert duties with the F-16C/D on 1 April 1987.

To augment Royal Saudi Air Force air defence radar coverage during the Iran-Iraq war, four E-3 Sentry aircraft and crews from TAC's 552nd Airborne Warning and

'Salty Bees' were reconnaissance unit deployments and Salty Bee '84 saw TAC's 12th TRS, 67th TRW, deploy seventeen RF-4Cs from Bergstrom AFB, Texas, to Zweibrücken AB, West Germany, 16 May–14 June 1984. Here, a 12th TRS RF-4C (upper aircraft) is seen in formation with one of the resident 38th TRS, 26th TRW, RF-4Cs over Zweibrücken. Note that the USAFE RF-4C still retains 'SEA' camouflage, whilst the visiting TAC RF-4C is in the newer 'European I' camouflage. (NARA)

A TAC F-4E of the 334th TFS, 4th TFW, leads a pair of Kongelige Danske Flyvevåben (Royal Danish Air Force) F-16As. The former was one of twelve 334th TFS F-4Es deployed from Seymour-Johnson AFB to Karup AB, Denmark, for Coronet Mariner from 29 April to 21 May 1987. (NARA)

Coronet Phaser, held 24 September–20 October 1987, was a large deployment, involving around twenty-four F-15C/Ds of both the 58th TFS and 60th TFS of the 33rd TFW from Eglin AFB, Florida, deploying to the Canadian Forces Base at Lahr, West Germany. Here a pair of 58th TFS F-15Cs, the nearest one with squadron commander's markings, fly past Burg Hohenzollern on 9 October 1987. (NARA)

The 107th TFS, 127th TFW, of the Michigan ANG deployed eleven A-7Ds and a single A-7K from Selfridge ANGB to Gioia Del Colle AB, Italy, from 4 to 23 May 1987 for Coronet Eclipse. Here one of the deployed Michigan ANG A-7Ds is seen in the slot position of a diamond formation led by an Aeronautica Militare Italiana (Italian Air Force) Tornado IDS, with an Italian F-104S to the left and a Türk Hava Kuvvetleri (Turkish Air Force) TF-104G to the right. The A-7D was taking part in NATO exercise Dragon Hammer '87 whilst deployed under Coronet Eclipse. It wears the then-usual ANG A-7 camouflage scheme which was similar to 'European I', but consisting of just grey and green, rather than the three-tone grey/dark green/medium green of 'European I'. (NARA)

Coronet Stone saw the deployment of eleven A-7Ds and a single A-7K of the 175th TFS, 114th TFG, South Dakota ANG, from Sioux Falls to Brustem AB, Belgium, from 2 to 23 September 1988. Here, three of the deployed A-7Ds are seen in formation with an early production F-16B (as shown by its small-area all-moving tailplane) of the Belgische Luchtmacht/Force Aérienne Belge (Belgian Air Force) during 'Cold Fire', which formed part of the Reforger '88 exercises. In the late 1980s, ANG A-7s switched from the camouflage scheme seen in the previous image to the two-tone light/dark grey scheme seen here. (NARA)

The 141st TFS, 108th TFG, New Jersey ANG, deployed from McGuire AFB to Bodø AB, Norway, for Coronet Garter from 12 to 24 September 1989 with twelve F-4Es. Here, one of the deployed F-4Es is seen in formation with a Luftforsvaret (Royal Norwegian Air Force) F-16B Block 15 OCU – this was actually the very last F-16 delivered to Norway, one of a pair of US-built F-16B attrition replacements received in 1989; all previous Norwegian F-16s were European-built. The F-4E is participating in exercise Barfrost '89 whilst deployed for Coronet Garter. (NARA)

Control Wing deployed to Riyadh under 'ELF One' (European Liaison Force One) in September 1980. KC-135 tankers also deployed in support. The eight-year deployment was under USAFE control initially, passing to United States Central Command Air Forces (USCENTAF) upon the latter's creation on 1 January 1983.

As noted previously, ANG and AFRES KC-135 tankers were also often deployed to Europe.

Electronic Security Command (ESC)

ESC monitored, collected and interpreted the military voice and electronic signals of countries of interest. Its European Electronic Security Division at Ramstein oversaw the 690th Electronic Security Wing (ESW) (Tempelhof Central Airport, West Berlin), the 691st ESW (Lindsey AS) and the 693rd ESW (RAF Chicksands). The latter controlled the 6950th Electronic Security Group (ESG) at Chicksands and 6917th ESG at San Vito dei Normanni AS, Italy, both operating distinctive AN/FLR-9 Wullenweber high-frequency direction-finding antenna arrays, and part of a worldwide 'Iron Horse' network of seven such arrays. A third AN/FLR-9 was at Augsburg in West Germany under 691st ESW control. A fourth at Karamursel AB, Turkey, had been deactivated and dismantled in 1977.

A 1989 aerial view of the 'Elephant Cage', as the AN/FLR-9 'Wullenweber' antenna array was known, at RAF Chicksands. Part of a global network of such arrays, known as 'Iron Horse', they were used for high-frequency direction finding under the control of Electronic Security Command. The AN/FLR-9 array at Chicksands was operated by the 6950th Electronic Security Group, 693rd Electronic Security Wing, of ESC's European Electronic Security Division. USAFE's 7274th Air Base Group provided logistic and administrative support. (NARA)

Into Action – Operation El Dorado Canyon

US-Libyan relations deteriorated during the 1980s due to Colonel Gaddafi's terrorism sponsorship; the first clash arose when USN F-14s shot down a pair of Libyan Su-22Ms in 1981. Contingency plans for striking Libyan facilities were prepared; with B-52s and F-117s ruled out, 48th TFW F-111Fs flying from the UK via France were chosen for any strike, alongside USN carrier strikes. Other F-111 wings supported the planning. The 20th TFW conducted Operation Ghost Rider on 18 October 1985, their F-111Es flying from Upper Heyford to hit a target near CFB Goose Bay in Canada 3,000 miles away, with refuelling support from seventeen tankers. Bombing by radar in darkness, more than half the bombs hit the target within seconds of the planned time-on-target. Innovations were made, including operating in formations of four aircraft (rather than the usual pairs), each four-ship having a dedicated tanker. In February 1986 eight 27th TFW F-111Ds flew from Cannon AFB, NM (joined near Mountain Home AFB, ID, by 390th ECS EF-111As), to a target near Eglin AFB, FL. The lessons from these exercises fed into the planning.

Further clashes with the USN in March 1986 and terrorist attacks in early April brought things to a head. Prime Minister Thatcher approved the mission being flown from the UK; however, France, Spain and Italy denied overflight rights, adding 1,300 miles each way to the journey. The F-111Fs now had to go around continental Europe, a 15-hour round-trip. Twenty-four KC-10As joined the existing ETTF KC-135 contingent; the concurrent NATO exercise Salty Nation was used to explain their presence. Reconnaissance was conducted by RC-135s, SR-71As and U-2Rs plus USN aircraft. HH-53Cs and HC-130Ns of 67th ARRS deployed to Naples to provide CSAR coverage.

Attack orders were received on 10 April for a 15 April mission. The final plan for 'Operation El Dorado Canyon' would see USAF aircraft co-ordinating with USN aircraft from the carriers *Coral Sea* and *America*. Whilst USN fighters provided top cover, stand-off support would be provided by TAC E-3As, USN E-2Cs and EA-3Bs. USN A-6Es would hit targets to the east (Benghazi barracks and Benina airfield) whilst Hornets/Corsairs conducted SEAD strikes and EA-6Bs escort jamming.

Simultaneously, eighteen F-111Fs, in six flights of three aircraft, would hit targets in the west; nine ('Remit', 'Elton' and 'Karma' Flights) attacking Bab al-Azizia complex (including Gaddafi's residence) with 2,000 lb GBU-10 LGBs, three ('Jewel') attacking Murat Sidi Bilal terrorist training camp with GBU-10s and six ('Puffy' and 'Lujac') targeting Tripoli airport (the former USAFE Wheelus AB) with Mk 82AIR 500 lb retarded bombs. Aircraft would not drop their bombs in the event of target uncertainty or weapons system problems. Each flight would launch with a fourth air-spare aircraft that would turn back if not required. Twenty-four of the 48th FW's most reliable aircraft were prepared for the mission. 'Harpo' Flight, five EF-111As (including an air-spare) from Upper Heyford, would support the F-111Fs. Each flight had a dedicated KC-10A tanker (one, 'Dobey-81', carrying Colonel Westbrook, 48th TFW, and mission, commander). These were in turn refuelled by a further twelve KC-10As and ten KC-135As.

At sunset on 14 April 1986, the F-111Fs took off with 30 seconds' separation – in radio-silence, with no flight plan and IFF turned off. Disaster was narrowly averted when some nearly collided with four RAF Tornados over RAF Honington. From Upper Heyford twenty F-111Es took off on a 'Salty Nation' mission as cover and EF-111As launched, joining the F-111Fs. Two F-111Fs developed faults and were replaced by air-spares. Many of the crews were not only refuelling from KC-10As for the first time, but at night and in radio silence.

Hours later, approaching western Sicily having travelled around Europe, Italian F-104S interceptors scrambled to identify the formation; intercepted by USN F-14As, they were told to move away. Word was passed to Italian Prime Minister Craxi, who advised his Maltese opposite number. He in turn tipped off Libyan authorities and Gaddafi and his family were rushed from the Bab al-Azizia complex with minutes to spare. Despite this warning, Libyan defences were caught by surprise.

Some of the F-111Fs were still refuelling during the final 'plug' as their tanking orbit circled to the north. Consequently, 'Elton 44' was too far north after refuelling to make its attack time-slot, becoming the first to abort. The remainder headed to their targets. The EF-111As dropped to 200 feet to provide close-in low-altitude jamming; however, 'Harpo-72' suffered a TFR or INS malfunction, the crew deciding to provide stand-off, high-altitude jamming instead.

The F-111Fs dropped to 200 feet, maintaining 600 knots with afterburner due to unexpected headwinds and the drag of their extended Pave Tack pods. The first of the F-111F crews crossed the Libyan coast at 0152 hrs, witnessing the last of the USN A-7Es firing ARMs at Libyan air defences.

At Bab al-Azizia the F-111Fs approached with 45-second separation, odd numbered call-signs offset left, even right, preventing their TFRs interfering with each other. Remit-31 and -33 dropped their GBU-10s short of Gaddafi's HQ, Remit-32 aborted after misidentifying its offset point. Remit-33 accelerated to 660 knots when a SAM was fired towards them as they headed back out to sea; when asked, during debrief, why he flew at 660 knots the pilot responded, 'Because it wouldn't do 661 knots'! No Elton flight aircraft bombed the target – all aborted with technical problems, one having to divert to Rota. Karma-51's crew inadvertently selected the wrong offset point and their four GBU-10s fell well off-target, hitting a civilian area, causing heavy damage to the French Embassy and killing Libyan civilians. Ironically, a senior member of the Abu Nidal terrorist group was also killed – an unintended success of the attacks. Libyan defences were now awake. A SAM site managed to lock on to Karma-51 despite jamming, but it was not hit. However, Karma-52, next approaching the target, was seen to hit the sea in a fireball. It was likely shot down by a SAM, possibly after an ALQ-131 ECM pod malfunction; ECM pods, being buffeted at high speed and at low level, received considerable punishment, several failing; some even fell apart. Pilot Captain Fernando Ribas-Dominici and WSO Captain Paul Lorence were tragically killed.

Last was Karma-53, but a Pave Tack generator failure forced them to abort and dump their bombs at sea. The Bab al-Azizia attack was largely a failure.

At Murat Sidi Bilal, Jewel-61 took evasive action due to accurate AAA fire and had target identification difficulties; its GBU-10s landed in a field. Jewel-62's crew located their target with Pave Tack; their four GBU-10s narrowly missed the target. Finally, despite dust and smoke interrupting its laser guidance, Jewel-63 successfully hit a frogman training pool and several boats.

Puffy and Lujac Flights had mediocre results at Tripoli airport, apart from the first jet over the target; Puffy-11 dropped its load of twelve Mk 82AIR bombs, destroying a pair of IL-76 transports, the consequent fire engulfing a second pair and damaging a fifth. Puffy-12 aborted, Puffy-13 missed the target and Lujac-22 and -23 both missed their target and jettisoned their bombs over the sea. A weapons computer software problem caused Lujac-24 to unload its Mk 82AIRs a mile short of the target.

The USN A-6Es hitting the targets to the east had more success. As the F-111Fs and EF-111As came off target, they passed over a destroyer acting as a 'delousing' ship at an agreed course, speed and altitude, and through the USN Tomcat/Hornet air defence screen, the latter approached to individually check the USAFE jets, ensuring no Libyan interceptors were taking advantage of the post-strike chaos to infiltrate the formations. Whilst at least two MiG-25s did scramble, none crossed the coastline. All aircraft successfully refuelled; however, they did not immediately return home, instead orbiting for nearly an hour in the hope that Karma-52 would reappear. At sunrise Col. Westbrook ordered a return to base.

Operation El Dorado Canyon, 1986: a 495th TFS, 48th TFW, F-111F, armed with 2,000 lb GBU-10 LGBs, prepares to launch as part of the strike package heading to Libya from RAF Lakenheath late on 14 April. This aircraft was 'Remit 31', from one of the flights which struck the Bab al-Azizia complex. 'Remit 31' dropped its LGBs just short of Gaddafi's HQ. (NARA)

The crew of a 48th TFW F-111F get the thumbs up before launching on their long journey to Libya during Operation El Dorado Canyon. (NARA)

Libya claimed thirty-seven civilian deaths, although some may have been caused by falling Libyan SAMs and AAA. Gaddafi also falsely claimed his adopted daughter had been killed in the raid. The F-111s arrived back at base after 14 hours and 35 minutes – although some crews were strapped in for 16 hours. This was far longer than the 2–3-hour missions the F-111 was designed for, causing the high proportion of systems failures and aborts. However, the mission was deemed a success and a great achievement by those involved. The operation marked the start of a more concerted US and international response to terrorism, Libya becoming increasingly isolated.

Det 4, 9th SRW, SR-71s made post-strike battle-damage assessment flights, finally getting images on the 17th (cloud frustrating earlier efforts), whilst on 7 September 1986 John F. Lehman, Secretary of the Navy, made the first inter-service award of the Navy Meritorious Unit Citation to the 48th TFW.

End of an Era

The fall of the Berlin Wall in 1989 and German reunification in 1990 heralded an abrupt end to the Cold War. Immediately, the possibility of a 'peace dividend' resulted in major defence cuts. Combined with the evaporating threat in Europe, USAFE was particularly hard hit.

Plans for deactivating many USAFE units got rapidly underway. The Gulf War would interrupt the drawdown, many USAFE units deploying to the Middle East to take part in Operations Desert Shield/Storm before standing down. The 1992 reorganisation of the USAF affected USAFE too, with supporting transports and tankers now directly assigned. By 1995 USAFE consisted of just one KC-135R, one F-15C/D and two F-15E squadrons in the UK, two F-16C/D squadrons in Italy and one OA/A-10A, three F-16C/D and three transport squadrons in Germany.

Bibliography

Bell, Dana, *USAF Colors and Markings in the 1990s* (London: Lionel Leventhal Limited, 1992)

Donald, David (ed.) *US Air Force Air Power Directory* (London: Aerospace Publishing Limited, 1992)

Francillon, René J., *The United States Air National Guard* (London: Aerospace Publishing Limited, 1993)

Gordon, Yefim and Dmitriy Komissarov, *Soviet Tactical Aviation* (Manchester: Hikoki Publications Limited, 2011)

Hopkins III, Robert S., *The Boeing KC-135 Stratotanker: More Than a Tanker* (Manchester: Crécy Publishing Limited, 2018)

Isby, David C. and Charles Kamps Jr, *Armies of NATO's Central Front* (London: Jane's Publishing Company Limited, 1985)

Lake, Jon (ed.), *McDonnell F-4 Phantom: Spirit in the Sky* (London: Aerospace Publishing Limited, 1992)

Marsh, Peter R., *Military Aircraft Markings* (Runnymede: Ian Allan Limited, 1980, 1981, 1982, 1985 and 1989 editions)

Martin, Patrick, *Tail Code: The Complete History of USAF Tactical Aircraft Tail Code Markings* (Atglen: Schiffer Publishing Limited, 1994)

Peake, William R., *McDonnell Douglas F-4 Phantom II Production and Operational Data* (Hinckley: Midland Publishing, 2004)

Rogers, Brian, *United States Air Force Unit Designations since 1978* (Hinckley: Midland Publishing, 2005)

Skinner, Michael, *USAFE: A Primer on Modern Air Combat in Europe* (London: Arms and Armour Press, 1988)

Thornborough, Anthony M. and Peter E. Davies, *The Phantom Story* (London: Arms and Armour Press, 1994)

Wright, Kevin, *The Collectors: US and British Cold War Aerial Intelligence Gathering* (Warwick: Helion & Company Limited, 2018)

Yenne, Bill, *The Complete History of US Cruise Missiles* (Forest Lake: Specialty Press, 2018)

Journals and Periodicals

United States Air Forces in Europe Yearbook 1989 and *Yearbook 1990* (IAT Publishing)

World Air Power Journal, various volumes (Aerospace Publishing Limited)

Unpublished Papers

Dellavolpe, Major David A., *History of Bardenas Reales Air-to-Ground Range 1970–1985* (Maxwell AFB: Air Command and Staff College, Air University, 1988)

Stiles, Gerald J., *The Wild Weasel Development Programs: One Run, One Hit, One Error* (Santa Monica: The RAND Corporation, 1990)

Appendix I

USAFE Structure 1980

USAFE HQ, Ramstein AB, West Germany

Direct Reporting:
7575th OG (Rhein-Main AB, West Germany)
7th SOS – MC-130E Combat Talon I
7405th OS – C-130E

3 AF, RAF Mildenhall, England

10th TRW (RAF Alconbury)
1st TRS – RF-4C ('AR' / blue)
527th TFTAS – F-5E

20th TFW (RAF Upper Heyford, 'UH')
55th TFS – F-111E (blue)
77th TFS – F-111E (red)
79th TFS – F-111E (yellow)

48th TFW (RAF Lakenheath, 'LN')
492nd TFS – F-111F (blue)
493rd TFS – F-111F (yellow)
494th TFS – F-111F (red)
495th TFS – F-111F (green)

81st TFW (RAF Bentwaters, 'WR')
78th TFS – A-10A (RAF Woodbridge) (red)
91st TFS – A-10A (RAF Woodbridge) (blue)
92nd TFS – A-10A (yellow)
509th TFS – A-10A (grey)
510th TFS – A-10A (purple)
511th TFS – A-10A (black)

513th TAW (RAF Mildenhall)
10th ACCS – EC-135H 'Silk Purse'

16 AF, Torrejon AB, Spain

401st TFW (Torrejon AB, 'TJ')
612th TFS – F-4D (blue/white)
613th TFS – F-4D (yellow/black)
614th TFS – F-4D (red/black)

406th TFTW (Zaragoza AB) [1]
40th TG (Aviano AB) [1]
7206th ABG (Hellenikon AB) [1]
HQ TUSLOG (Ankara AS)
TUSLOG Det 10 (Incirlik AB) [1]

17 AF, Sembach AB, West Germany

Direct Reporting:
32d TFS – F-15A/B [2] (Soesterberg AB, Netherlands, 'CR', orange)

26th TRW (Zweibrücken AB, 'ZR')
38th TRS – RF-4C (green/white checkerboard)

36th TFW (Bitburg AB, 'BT')
22d TFS – F-15A/B [2] (red)
53d TFS – F-15A/B [2] (yellow/black tiger stripes)
525th TFS – F-15A/B [2] (blue)

50th TFW (Hahn AB, 'HR')
10th TFS – F-4E (blue)
313th TFS – F-4E (white)
496th TFS – F-4E (red)

52nd TFW (Spangdahlem AB, 'SP')
23d TFS – F-4D [3] (blue)
81st TFS – F-4G (yellow)

480th TFS – F-4D/E [4] (red)

86th TFW (Ramstein AB, 'RS')
512th TFS – F-4E (yellow/black checkerboard)
526th TFS – F-4E (red/black checkerboard)

601st TCW (Sembach AB)
601st TASG
20th TASS – OV-10A
704th TASS – OV-10A
601st TASS – CH-53C

Strategic Air Command in Europe

7th Air Division (Ramstein AB, West Germany)

Direct Reporting:
34th SS (Zaragoza AB, Spain) – TDY KC-135

306th SW – TDY KC-135 and RC-135 (RAF Mildenhall, UK)
922d SS – TDY KC-135 (Hellenikon AB, Greece)

11th SG – TDY KC-135 (RAF Fairford)
Det, 11th SG – TDY KC-135 (Keflavik, Iceland)

9th SRW (Beale Air Force Base, CA)
OL-OH [5] – TDY U-2R (RAF Akrotiri, Cyprus)
Det 4, HQ, 9th SRW – TDY U-2R, occasional SR-71A deployments (RAF Mildenhall, UK)

Military Airlift Command in Europe

21 AF, McGuire AFB, NJ

322nd Airlift Division (Ramstein AB, West Germany)
Direct Reporting:
58th MAS – C-12A, C-135B, VC-140B, CT-39A (Ramstein AB)

435th TAW (Rhein-Main AB)
37th TAS – C-130E
55th AAS – C-9A
Det 1, HQ, 435th TAW – C-9A (VIP) (Chièvres AB)

313th TAG – TDY C-130E/H (RAF Mildenhall, UK)

39th ARRW (Eglin AFB, Florida)
67th ARRS – HC-130H/N/P, HH-53C (RAF Woodbridge)
Det 2, 67th ARRS – UH-1N (Ramstein)
Det 9, 67th ARRS – UH-1N (Zaragoza)
Det 14, 67th ARRS – HH-3E (Keflavik)

Air Force Communications Command in Europe
1868th FCS – T-39A (Rhein Main AB)

Notes:
1) No aircraft permanently assigned
2) Upgraded to F-15C/D during 1980
3) Started to receive some F-4Es from 4/80
4) Last F-4D left 3/80 when replaced by F-4E
5) Became 'Det 3, HQ, 9th SRW' 9/80

USAFE Structure 1989

USAFE HQ, Ramstein AB, West Germany

Direct Reporting:
7575th OG (Rhein-Main AB, West Germany)
7405th OS – C-130E

3 AF, RAF Mildenhall, England

10th TFW (RAF Alconbury, 'AR')
509th TFS – A-10A (grey)
511th TFS – A-10A (black)

20th TFW (RAF Upper Heyford, 'UH')
55th TFS – F-111E (blue)
77th TFS – F-111E (red)
79th TFS – F-111E (yellow)
(Attached squadron: 42nd ECS – EF-111A; see 66th ECW, 17 AF)

48th TFW (RAF Lakenheath, 'LN')
492nd TFS – F-111F (blue)
493rd TFS – F-111F (yellow)
494th TFS – F-111F (red)
495th TFS – F-111F (green)

81st TFW (RAF Bentwaters, 'WR')
78th TFS – A-10A (RAF Woodbridge) (red)
91st TFS – A-10A (RAF Woodbridge) (blue)
92nd TFS – A-10A (yellow)
510th TFS – A-10A (purple)
527th AS – F-16C Block (red)

513th ACCW (RAF Mildenhall)
10th ACCS – EC-135H 'Silk Purse', WC-135B

303rd TMW [1] (RAF Molesworth)
87th TMS [1] – BGM-109G

501st TMW (RAF Greenham Common)
11th TMS – BGM-109G

16 AF, Torrejón AB, Spain

401st TFW (Torrejón AB, 'TJ')
612th TFS – F-16C/D Block 30 (blue/white checkerboard)
613th TFS – F-16C/D Block 30 (yellow/black checkerboard)
614th TFS – F-16C/D Block 30 (red/black checkerboard)

487th TMW (Comiso AB)
302nd TMS – BGM-109G

406th TFTW (Zaragoza AB) [2]
40th TG (Aviano AB) [2]
7206th ABG (Hellenikon AB) [2]
HQ TUSLOG (Ankara AS)
39th TG (Incirlik AB) [2]

17 AF, Sembach AB, West Germany

Direct Reporting:
32d TFS [3] – F-15C/D (Soesterberg AB, Netherlands, 'CR', orange)

26th TRW (Zweibrücken AB, 'ZR')
38th TRS – RF-4C (green/white checkerboard)

36th TFW (Bitburg AB, 'BT')
22d TFS – F-15C/D (red)

53d TFS – F-15C (yellow / black tiger stripes)
525th TFS – F-15C/D (blue)

50th TFW (Hahn AB, 'HR')
10th TFS – F-16C/D Block 25 (blue)
313th TFS – F-16C/D Block 25 (orange)
496th TFS – F-16C/D Block 25 (yellow)

38th TMW (Wüschheim AS)
89th TMS – BGM-109G

485th TMW [4] (Florennes AB, Belgium)
71st TMS [5] – BGM-109G

65th Air Division (Lindsey AS)

52nd TFW (Spangdahlem AB, 'SP')
23rd TFS – F-4G, F-16C/D Block 30 (blue)
81st TFS – F-4G, F-16C/D Block 30 (yellow)
480th TFS – F-4G, F-16C/D Block 30 (red)

66th ECW (Sembach AB, 'SB')
42d ECS – EF-111A (Detached to 3 AF/20th TFW, RAF Upper Heyford)
43d ECS – EC-130H Compass Call

601st TCW (Sembach AB) (non-flying)

316th Air Division (Ramstein AB)

86th TFW (Ramstein AB, 'RS')
512th TFS – F-16C/D Block 30 (green/black stripes)
526th TFS – F-16C/D Block 30 (red/black stripes)

Strategic Air Command in Europe

7th Air Division (Ramstein AB)

17th RW (RAF Alconbury, UK)
95th RS – TR-1A

306th SW – TDY KC-135s and RC-135s (RAF Mildenhall, UK)
922d SS – TDY KC-135s (Hellenikon AB, Greece)
Det 1, HQ, 306th SW – TDY KC-135 (Keflavik, Iceland)

11th SG – TDY KC-135s (RAF Fairford)
34th SS – TDY KC-10A (Zaragoza)

9th SRW (Beale AFB, CA)
Det 3, HQ, 9th SRW – TDY U-2R (RAF Akrotiri, Cyprus)
Det 4, HQ, 9th SRW – TDY SR-71A (RAF Mildenhall, UK)

Military Airlift Command in Europe

21 AF, McGuire AFB, NJ

322nd Airlift Division (Ramstein AB)

435th TAW (Rhein-Main AB)
37th TAS – C-130E
55th AAS – C-9A
Det 1, HQ, 435th TAW – C-9A (VIP) (Chievres AB)

313th TAG – TDY C-130E/H (RAF Mildenhall, UK)

608th MAG (Ramstein AB)
10th MAS – C-23A (Zweibrücken AB)
58th MAS – C-12F, C-20A, C-21A, T-43A, C-135B, UH-1N (Ramstein AB)

23 AF, Hurlburt Field, FL [6]

39th SOW (Rhein-Main AB)
7th SOS – MC-130E Combat Talon I (Rhein-Main AB)
21st SOS – MH-53J, HH-53B, CH-53C (RAF Woodbridge)
67th SOS – HC-130H/N/P (RAF Woodbridge)

375th AAW (Scott AFB, IL)
Detachment 2, 1467th FCS – T-39A
  (Rhein Main Air Base)

Air Rescue Service, McClellan AFB, CA [6]

56th ARS – HH-3E (Keflavik, Iceland)

Notes:
1) Inactivated 31 Jan 89.
2) No aircraft permanently assigned.

3) 32nd TFS reassigned to newly formed
  32nd TFG, 16 Nov 89.
4) Inactivated 30 Sept 89.
5) Inactivated 30 Apr 89.
6) 23 AF and Air Rescue Service structure
  shown for late-89 after restructuring
  throughout the year.